S5

SENTENTIA
THE JOURNAL

Paula Bomer, Publisher

Guest Editor and designer:
  Adam Robinson

Cover Painting:
  Jonathan Allen

ISBN 13: 978-0-9838790-6-0

www.SententiaBooks.com

Sententia is Latin for sentence, but also means thought, meaning, and purpose, all of which are relevant to the work we seek to publish. Sententia embraces the traditional and experimental in narrative, both in our books as well as in *Sententia: The Journal*. Submission guidelines and other information can be found at the website.

Sententia 4 was edited by Amy King and Jen Michalski. Past issues are available at the website.

a way of
thinking opinion meaning
and **purpose**

Sententia 5

Pushing Fifty at the 7-11

JP Reese

Today, I turn forty-nine, and I'm standing behind the counter, rows and rows of cigarettes lining the wall behind my head. It's not Wednesday, my free day, and Sanjay's wife told him there was no way I was getting extra time off, so here I am, smiling at truckers and high school punks from behind this Plexiglas on my birthday.

Sanjay told me this morning I've still got it, right before he gave me the black balloons and devil's food cupcake, but at my age, I know the Maybelline really doesn't cover the years like it used to. Seems like every morning gravity pulls each new wrinkle into a sad clown face, so I avoid mirrors except when I'm flossing, I eat bran to stay regular, and I never believe what Sanjay tells me. He's a terrible flirt.

Mama quit smoking ten years before she got sick, but I still like a Pall Mall with my evening rum and Coke, and Nicorette is so damned expensive. I stick to her brand out of loyalty and because we sell them cheap here at the store. When mom went two years back, I sold all her books to the Half-Price book store the week after she died and got enough cash back for a couple cartons of cigarettes. The job here at 7-11 barely covers the mortgage, so a carton is a big deal around my house. His wife doesn't like it, but Sanjay gives me an employee discount too, so it's a good deal all around.

When I got laid off from the John Deere two years ago, I lost my health insurance, and I've been dipping into my 401K to keep the house. I keep telling myself it's too big for just me, but it still smells like Mama, and I can't get myself to part with some of her furniture yet. I don't have parties like I used to when I worked at Deere. All my friends at the plant who still have their jobs don't call anymore. I guess they think getting laid off's contagious. I'm really pretty lucky Sanjay offered me the cashier's job, even though it's only minimum wage. If I'm real careful, I can keep going for at least another year or two before my retirement's all gone and then there's only fifteen years until social security kicks in. I'm keeping an eye on that little lump under my arm, too, but I'm sure it's just a cyst or something. It'd be dumb to spend money on a doctor for a little bump that's not going to kill me.

Sanjay keeps telling me I should ask him over, then he raises those bushy eyebrows and makes a hissing noise between his teeth, like he doesn't mean it, but he does. He never actually asks me out anywhere or calls unless that kid Walter doesn't show up for his shift. He says his wife doesn't understand him, and that's plain for anyone to see, but I'm a little scared of her with all those orange silk wrappers and that red dot on her forehead. Besides, these days my do-it motor's lugging down to a funny whine, so even though the phone never rings, *Dancing with the Stars* is on every Wednesday to keep me company when I settle into Mama's favorite reading chair and flip through the channels.

Some nights, I wake in the bed I've slept in practically all my life, and in that moment between waking and sleep, a fifteen-year-old me stands in the doorway, her back turned, the world spread before her like a hotel banquet table covered with great food. When I look over her shoulder, I see fancy place cards shaped like airplane seats, all of them labeled with my name. Then she turns around to face me, and I see only empty black holes where her eyes ought to be and a big orange dot in the middle of her forehead, just like Sanjay's wife, but this one's on fire, like the tail end of a Pall Mall smoking between Mama's fingers, or the laser on a sniper's site, aiming straight down the covers at me.

The Aardvark

Josh Ostergaard

It was their last day in Durban, and while his wife Stefanie was busy finishing medical meetings, Mark traveled an hour from the city to visit the Valley of a Thousand Hills. A Zulu village was open for tourists a short walk from a reptile park.

Mark left the minibus driver in the parking lot and walked toward the huts. He paused near the entrance to a round hut with a grass roof and took his camera from his bag. An attractive black woman wearing a pale yellow blouse and a beige skirt stepped inside its open door. She wore the uniform of the catering staff at his hotel. Mark pretended to fiddle with his camera bag as the woman removed her cherry-colored shoes and stood barefoot on the hut's dirt floor. She unbuttoned her blouse and removed her brassiere. As she gripped the zipper on the back of her skirt, she turned and looked his way. Their eyes met.

An hour later, during the dances, Mark saw her in the middle of the long row of topless Zulu women wearing grass skirts. She was a bit plump for his taste, but he snapped a picture anyway. After the dance, Mark trudged up an asphalt hill to the reptile park and stared at deadly ash-gray mambas lying entwined behind glass.

* * *

In the morning they climbed into a Mercedes and drove out of Durban toward Swaziland. Mark had convinced Stefanie to take advantage of being in South Africa and not work the whole time. He had researched private game reserves for them to visit, and they'd invited along Stefanie's senior colleague, Dr. Hoost, who was as thin as a hospital patient even though he could eat four langoustines and a steak without taking a breath. Just outside the city they passed a billboard with a picture of a condom on it, and Dr. Hoost laughed and told them fifty thousand had been dispersed across the countryside with instructions stapled through the middle. "Our public health system," he said. "Nobody noticed in time."

During their short stay in Durban, police had kidnapped two men from the beach in front of their hotel, and a child had stabbed eleven others with a needle. Mark had been told South African roads were even more dangerous than its cities, but this road was well cared for. The blacktop was smooth and the highway's lanes were separated by a grassy median. He sensed what Stefanie was thinking in the front seat. With roads this good it would be easy for medicine to reach small towns and people living in the bush. She was never able to set aside her medical perspective, her impulse to act, to take charge, even after her meetings ended. Mark, a theoretical physicist, could not imagine why Stefanie enjoyed dealing with people day after day. The universe didn't need humanity. He'd been denied tenure a year before and had taken work as a public education specialist at a planetarium. The hair along his temples had speckled gray and he'd been over-served at local bars countless times, yet Mark felt he was handling his professional transition well. Time once spent exploring the mysteries of the universe had been replaced by a bland recitation of facts for sweaty groups of hungry children on field trips. The earth revolved around the sun three times a day. Every day. Sometimes on weekends. Over time a curious need burned within him and he longed to tell the children the sun revolved around the earth. They would believe it—they believed everything he said. Rather than respecting their innocence, it grew to annoy him, and his irritation bled into his befuddlement at Stefanie's professional obsession with helping everyone.

They stopped for lunch at an America-themed burger stand off the highway. Marilyn Monroe, Barack Obama, and Ernest Hemingway were painted on a wall. Afterward, they passed grass huts to the left where Mark supposed more Zulus lived. The image of the woman changing out of her street clothes simmered in his mind. They passed yellow trees, which Dr. Hoost called fever trees because their bark was an old remedy for malaria before the Europeans arrived with their quinine-laced tonic. Finally they saw their first giraffe standing with its head stretched skyward, legs spread for balance.

* * *

After they checked in a Zulu man introduced himself. Aaron's build was sturdy and short, and the collar of his shirt was stained with dried sweat. He would be their tracker on game drives, which meant he'd sit in a higher seat in the front of the Land Rover and spot animals with a scope. His khaki safari clothes were exactly what Mark had imagined. To his surprise Aaron also carried a machine gun over his shoulder as he walked them to their private lodges in a sand forest. Aaron told a story about a German tourist killed the year before. She'd been walking this same path alone when she was taken by a lion. Mark shuddered and grabbed hold of Stefanie's hand. "The only lions we've got in Chicago are in a museum diorama," he said.

"You may also see an elephant in these woods," Aaron said. "Be careful."

Mark saw their lodge through the trees. Its walls were glass, and as they approached they saw its ceiling was also glass. The forest canopy had been cut away to allow for a view of the stars at night from inside.

After Aaron left to guide Dr. Hoost to his own lodge further into the forest, Stefanie and Mark stood encased in glass without speaking. They set down their things and looked around. There was a bottle of champagne chilling in a silver ice bucket. Stefanie opened it and poured two glasses. A bowl of apples, oranges, bananas, and a green fruit neither of them recognized sat on the table next to the champagne. A noise near the front door caught their attention and they turned in time to see a large gray monkey run inside the room and grab Mark's camera from the table where he'd set it next to the fruit. The monkey turned, ran out the door, and shimmied up a tree. It stared at them, holding the silver box with its long thin fingers.

* * *

Later that afternoon Stefanie was in the shower and Mark crept from their lodge to look for his camera. The white sand was soft and deep between the trees. His whole body felt alert and alive. Mark veered to his right, walking carefully with his eyes searching the ground. It was autumn, and yellow leaves lay on the sand. Ahead, between two small groves, he saw the sun flash on metal. He snatched the camera.

Suddenly he heard an elephant trumpet nearby. It bellowed again, and this time it was closer. The sound was coming from above, as though it were a huge male, but no elephant was in sight. Mark walked toward the trees, and scanned the tall trunks and branches. The sound was so loud the elephant should have been close. Then he saw a small speaker affixed to a limb near the main trunk.

Mark snapped a picture of the speaker and walked back to the lodge. Stefanie had finished her shower and was still in the bathroom. He opened the door. Warm wet air billowed past his face and her blue eyes appeared in the mist. He held up the camera.

"Where -"

"The monkey brought it back," he said.

"You shouldn't go out there alone. Did you hear the elephant?"

"It was a speaker in a tree."

"Whatever." She smiled.

"I saw it myself." He showed her the picture.

"There's a simpler explanation." Having dismissed his worry, she leaned in close, kissed him, and said, "Don't go out there alone again."

* * *

Just before sunset Aaron appeared at their glass cabin with his machine gun and walked Mark and Stefanie to the Land Rover, where they joined Dr. Hoost and met their guide, a white man in his mid-thirties named Russell. The small group rode for half an hour along narrow dirt paths into a vast field. They stopped to drink gin and tonic and eat sandwiches of cured meats and pungent white cheese. The best game viewing was early morning and late evening, so they lingered until night overtook them.

Stefanie stood with her back to the group, looked toward the tall grass, and asked, "How well do lions see in the dark?"

Aaron said, "very well compared to us." He grinned.

"Are there lions nearby?"

"Yes," said Aaron.

Russell stacked meat and cheese onto a slab of dry bread, and told a story. "Ten years ago, I think it was. There was an attack in Kruger. All they found was binoculars and an ulna bone. It had been licked until its meat was gone. Rangers assumed it was lions, and issued a warning, but really there was nothing to be done."

"Nature," said Dr. Hoost. He motioned for Aaron to bring him more cheese, and Aaron did. Russell said, "It's not just hunger. Big cats are territorial, like people. Lions kill baby cheetahs to protect their hunting grounds."

When it was dark they walked together toward the Land Rover. Stefanie held the camera and flipped past images of the topless Zulu dancer and the trees and huts of the rural countryside before stopping on the speaker in the tree. "What's this for?" she asked Aaron, holding it for him to see.

Mark had been too wary to ask on his own, but now he added, "I saw it earlier today."

"The public address system," Aaron said. "In case we need to speak to the whole reserve at once. Like any big park. It's for staff." He smiled. "What did you think?"

"Nothing," Stefanie said, and softly punched Mark's arm.

"Mark," said Aaron, "be careful. Don't walk outside your lodge without me."

Mark felt maybe Aaron was right as he and Stefanie climbed into the back row of the open air seats. Dr. Hoost sat ahead of them, while Aaron and Russell were in the front. A CB was mounted between them, and when the truck was stopped a blast of static sometimes interrupted the quiet and the whole group listened. It was mostly in English, but other times it was in Afrikaans or Zulu so Dr. Hoost translated for the Americans. They had been traveling for fifteen minutes when Aaron yelled "Ahead to the right!" A round pink animal with a rat's tail, a pig's snout, and a rabbit's ears vanished into the brush. It was gone in a second, but everyone had seen it. Russell turned off the truck's engine so they could talk.

"Very hard to see an aardvark," Aaron said. "It's a shy animal."

Russell said, "If it was my job to take you to find the aardvark, I'd be out of work."

"It looked like a steamed prawn," Dr. Hoost said, a bit too loudly.

Mark hadn't come on a safari to look at aardvarks. He wanted to see cheetahs, water buffalo—something big enough to kill him given the chance. The aardvark looked vulnerable, like an armadillo without a shell. The Land Rover bumbled along a dirt path, and the tourists strained to see animals in Aaron's spotlight. The group was silent. The noise of the truck made it impossible to hear each other and speaking loudly might scare the game.

Stefanie clutched Mark's hand. The truck stopped where a line of trees met an open field. The engine knocked as it cooled. The slightest rustle of a leaf, the meanest shift in the way the insects hummed, now seemed charged with importance. There was no moon, and the stars were low and white. The darkness along the ground was total, and without the truck or the guides, Mark knew they would not last the night walking through the park.

Yip.

The sound was soft, as though the animal was too shy to commit to barking. Dr. Hoost whispered loudly enough for Stefanie and Mark to hear, "Wild dogs." It came from the field ahead of them. Aaron and Russell whispered to each other in voices too quiet for Mark to hear. Static burst from the CB, and Aaron leaned over to turn it down.

Yip.

Finally, Russell turned around and in a soft but clear voice addressed the tourists. "We've got cheetahs up here, one hundred meters ahead and fifty meters to the left off the trail. We're going to take a look—they sound like a brood of pups."

The Land Rover engine coughed as it started, and Mark feared it would scare the cheetahs before they could see them. The headlights bored into the night, and in his heightened state it looked to Mark as though the light was creating a new world as it traveled, and that all the blackness outside the beams was truly a void. The hiss and crunch of the tires across the earth was loud enough to obscure the yipping cheetahs. Suddenly the truck stopped.

Russell turned and said, "They're here—look at the far edge of our headlights, there on the right—see that round shape in the grass!"

A small cheetah cub looked directly into the truck's lights and its eyes glowed green. Three other cheetah cubs flopped out from behind a thick patch of grass, illuminated by the lights. The cheetah cubs stopped abruptly in the glare but seemed unafraid of the Land Rover. Dr. Hoost turned to Mark and said, "I've never seen cubs in the wild before, never heard them either. I've never been this close."

* * *

The next night there was a group dinner, and people were invited from all the different habitats in the park. The private game reserve was vast, and tourists picked between environments based on which animals they wanted to see. Now they all congregated for a feast. The party was held in a cozy banquet hall inside the main reception lodge, a hundred yards from the boma, where late-night drinks were often served around a bonfire. Mark and Stefanie arrived before Dr. Hoost, and after getting their drinks spotted Aaron, who waved them over.

"Your country is so beautiful," Stefanie said.

"She is," said Aaron. He was wearing a freshly pressed set of khakis.

"It must be great now that Apartheid is over," blurted Mark, and he knew it was the wrong thing immediately because Stefanie glared.

"Yes," said Aaron, "racism is gone now, just like in America." He laughed, and Stefanie and Mark joined him uneasily. The noise in the room had increased as guests arrived, and it was difficult to hear. Mark stood by in silence and hoped Dr. Hoost would arrive soon. He stirred his ice. The drink was already gone.

"What's your favorite animal?" asked Stefanie.

"If I had to choose it would be the one you've already seen."

"The cheetah?"

"The aardvark. They are harder to find than the others."

Mark excused himself to find the bathroom. Idle chatter was unbearable. He left the banquet room and walked down the hall, which was decorated with photographs from the different habitats in the reserve: swamp, desert, mountain, sand forest. He did not see a bathroom, but turned left and walked down another long hallway to waste more time before dinner. Along the way he passed a row of offices. A door was slightly ajar and Mark pushed it open. A park employee sat next to an array of audio equipment. He looked up in surprise, and Mark thought the young man didn't seem old enough to hold a job.

"Bathroom?" Mark asked.

"WC is the other way, on your right."

Before he turned away, Mark noticed a map of the park glowing brightly on the computer screen. When he returned to the banquet room he found Dr. Hoost, Stefanie, and Aaron talking about the local kingfisher population.

"There you are," said Dr. Hoost. "I've found us a table." He led Mark and Stefanie across the crowded room. Aaron stayed behind. "You'll love the springbok steaks," Dr. Hoost said once they sat down. "They are my favorite wild game."

* * *

Later that night Stefanie lay deeply asleep but Mark was alert. The stars shined brightly through the ceiling. His eyes had adjusted to the dark, and in any direction he looked, he saw the silhouettes of the forest that surrounded their lodge. If an animal came close, he would see it.

A loud blast rattled the glass walls. Stefanie awoke. She slipped out of bed and walked to the window nearest the sound.

"Another elephant," she said.

Mark walked up and hugged her from behind. They stared into the dark at the outlines of the trees, looking for the animals.

"It's so crazy," Stefanie said quietly, "I can't believe there's nothing but glass between us and the wild."

* * *

By sunrise the next morning the group had been on the trail a half-hour. The goal, Russell said, was to find a pride of lions. After, they would try to get another look at the cheetahs, which were even more beautiful in the daylight. They passed giraffe, and then elephant, and several warthogs grazing in a field. Mark dutifully added them to the digital museum trapped inside his camera. Now they were his. The Land Rover stopped and everyone stared at a cluster of rhinoceros. They had tiny eyes, and their horns and thick skins made them look invulnerable. The group murmured quietly while they watched. Dr. Hoost offered that rhinoceros looked like dinosaurs, like triceratops without a shield behind their heads. "Biceratops," he joked, and then added they also looked like a species of beetle he'd seen in an old museum in Kuching, but he'd forgotten its name. Finally he had it. "Rhinoceros beetle," he said in triumph. Everyone laughed.

Russell said poaching was hurting the rhinoceros population, and not solely through the deaths of the animals by bullets. When mature elephants were poached for their tusks, younger, surviving male elephants became violent, aggressive, and prone to attack. And some of them began to rape rhinoceros to death. Nearly forty rhinoceros had been killed this way in recent years.

"Actually," Mark said, "The adult elephants were culled by biologists."

Russell frowned and said, "Well, yes, I suppose."

"I read it in the *Herald Tribune* in Durban," Mark continued. "Biologists thought it would be easier than moving them alive. We do it in the States with deer."

The CB static crinkled the air, and Aaron picked up the handle and spoke into it, then listened. Dr. Hoost turned to the others and said, "lions." He held his hand up for them to keep quiet, and he listened for a few more seconds. "It sounds like someone found lions, and Aaron thinks we can intercept them four kilometers from here."

Russell turned to the group and confirmed what Dr. Hoost had said, and added gravely that the lions were very near where the cheetah cubs had been seen. He started the engine and they drove away. Suddenly Russell swerved, and then corrected the truck.

"What was that?" asked Stefanie.

"Elephant dung," hollered Aaron over the engine. He turned around to explain. "Elephants eat vegetation with thorns big enough to puncture tires." This delighted Dr. Hoost and Stefanie, who shared jokes about the disadvantages of passing a thorn so big and sharp through a GI tract. Mark smiled. Stefanie's sense of humor was rarely as macabre as his, except when it came to bodily functions.

"There," said Aaron, and the truck lurched to a stop. The trees came to within ten feet on either side of the dirt track the Land Rover was using for a trail.

"What?" said Stefanie. The tourists didn't see anything. Aaron held up his hand. His gaze was focused on the trees to the right of the Land Rover, no more than five meters away.

The trees emitted a rustling sound, but Stefanie saw no lions. Neither did anyone else. A minute later the encounter was over. Russell and Aaron leaned in toward each other and murmured. Dr. Hoost turned to the others. "I can't hear them."

Russell turned and said, "It seems the lions are staying in the trees for now. Aaron is worried they may have molested the cheetahs we saw last night. Lions are so close to the cheetahs now it seems like a dangerous situation."

The Americans leaned in closer. Russell continued. "We'll go look and see if we can check on the cheetahs."

* * *

Mid-day was nap time. The early morning game drives, after-dark excursions, and festivities in the boma at night made guests sleepy during the day. Mark and Stefanie skipped the lunch buffet at the main lodge. Instead they had sex. In the daylight, within the glass, it felt like they were outside. Their limbs glistened like snakes as they slithered along and against each other. In the middle of it, Stefanie laughed and pointed at the ceiling. A large gray monkey sat on the glass roof, watching. Mark rolled over onto his back and pulled the sheet over them.

"It's no different than Rickey," Stefanie said. She kissed Mark's ear.

"It's thinking," Mark said. "Elkhounds don't think."

"Maybe it wishes it could take our picture," Stefanie said.

"Looks like it wants to join us," Mark said, and they both laughed. He kissed her neck.

After they'd untangled themselves, Stefanie got snacks from her suitcase and brought them back to bed to supplement their improvised lunch of fresh fruit. She brought string cheese, orange colored peanut butter crackers and, for dessert, a bag of animal cookies. Now they lay in bed and nibbled.

"A buffalo," Mark said, and bit its head off and chewed.

"A giraffe," Stefanie said, and chomped it to bits. A rhinoceros. A gazelle. Mark thought it strange there were no carnivores.

"A monkey!" Stefanie said, and she crunched its head. Their own monkey had jumped from the roof to the forest floor, but it was still watching.

The morning game drive worried them. They had found the young cheetahs near where they'd heard the lions, and had been thrilled to see them up close again. Cheetahs reminded Mark of dogs, the way the cubs loped around and roughhoused with each other. But the adult cheetahs were missing, and Russell had been concerned the lions may have killed them.

Stefanie plucked another animal cookie from the bag. It was an elephant. She scowled and pulverized the little elephant between her teeth. She leaned forward to stare between the trees.

"Hey, come back," said Mark, and he pulled her gently onto her pillow. Just then they heard a loud roar, a lion, and sat up in bed and looked toward the sound. They watched, but the sound didn't repeat and they couldn't see the lion. "The monkey's not afraid," said Mark. It sat in place on the ground, showing no sign of nervousness.

* * *

As they enjoyed their sunset cocktails on the veld, Russell and Aaron briefed the group. They had spoken with the other guides and trackers throughout the day, and it seemed the cheetah cubs were still alone and separated from their parents. It was unusual for cubs that young to be left for so long, even if the adults were away hunting. A dangerous situation. The cubs would surely be killed. The darkness settled and the moon was a thin, curved line. The group loaded into the truck to look for the cubs. Russell drove directly to the place where the cheetah pups were last seen. The insects hummed. Five minutes passed, or longer, and nobody spoke.

Stefanie gripped Mark's hand, and whispered, loudly, "I hope those cubs are okay."

Dr. Hoost turned and nodded. Aaron and Russell leaned close to each other and whispered quietly. The CB fizzed and garbled speech came through.

Russell turned to the others. "It's a bit unnerving, we'd expect the cubs to be here based on last reports."

The group fell silent. Mark strained to listen. The faintest sounds—the flap of a bird or a bat's wings, leaves ruffling gently in the woods—were amplified. Mark heard a faint scraping, so small it could not be a cheetah, but he was curious and peered over the edge of the Land Rover. He pointed a small flashlight toward the sound and saw a monstrous dung beetle near the rear tire. It was pushing a perfectly round ball of shit with its legs. It reminded him of Stefanie, taking the world's burdens upon herself, straining with futility against the relentless truth: everyone suffered, everyone died, and it did not matter.

The roar of a lion broke the silence.

Mark pulled back inside the Land Rover, terrified at the sound. Aaron held up his hand. A single minute passed slowly, while Mark realized it had been the first time he'd extended any part of his body beyond the interior of the Land Rover. He'd crossed an imaginary boundary. His fingers felt vulnerable. It was a thrill. He was almost giddy. The lion roared, louder, closer. It was on the move, heading west from east, but still in the distance.

Russell turned back toward the group and said quietly, "it's still a kilometer or so away, but it seems to be moving toward this area. We'll wait and list—"

A cheetah cub sounded from thick grass to the west of the Land Rover. Russell was silent. It sounded like there were at least two cubs yipping, perhaps more. Dr. Hoost said, "They sound scared!" The cheetah pups were two hundred meters away, or less. As the minutes passed their yips went further and further west.

The lion roared and snorted. It was closer, but not within sight.

Russell and Aaron whispered to each other, and Russell turned to speak to the group. "The cheetahs are moving toward an area of the park not accessible by Land Rover. The terrain may protect them from the lion."

Stefanie spoke. "So we just leave them? Alone?"

"Unfortunately, even if the cheetahs remained here we could do nothing to protect them," Russell said.

"We've got to do something. Aren't cheetahs endangered?"

Dr. Hoost put his hand on Stefanie's shoulder and spoke. "Lions are endangered. Should we shoot one animal to save another?"

Stefanie and Mark gripped each others' hands.

Russell said, "A shallow river expands in a bend into a large water hole four kilometers south of here. Good chance of seeing croc, hippo, and elephant all in one place so that's where we'll go. And keep your eyes open along the way."

* * *

At the boma that night, the talk among all the tourists was whether the cheetah pups would survive with the lions prowling after them and the parents missing. The interior was lined with torches that cast orange light onto the enclosure's wooden slats. A giant bonfire crackled. There were desserts arranged on trays near a vat of mulled wine, which Aaron scooped and served because a worker had skipped her shift. The air smelled of cloves.

Stefanie and Mark stood with Russell, discussing the chances the cheetah would live. "It sure is exciting though," said Stefanie.

"Yes," said Russell. "Nothing like animals in a zoo, is it? Here they are free to tear each other apart as they wish."

"That reminds me," Mark said. His words betrayed a light slur. "We aren't necessarily safe inside this boma. Remember the lions of Tsavo? In the museum back home. It was 1890-something and some workers were building a railroad in Tsavo, which is a part of South Africa—"

"Kenya," said Russell.

"Kenya. Two lions went on a rampage and killed dozens of people. For their meat. Workers built bomas from heavy sticks and thorny branches to protect themselves at night, but the lions still broke through. Usually they're afraid of fire, but they'd just dart toward a person and drag them back into the bush where it was dark."

Stefanie did not like the story. "That would never happen anymore."

An elderly couple appeared on the edge of their little circle just as Mark finished. Their faces were illuminated by the firelight. The smell of wood smoke filled the air.

"Good bit of drama tonight, haven't we?" said the woman. She had a British accent and wore large gold earrings with white diamonds in the center, while he was dressed in a formal blue jacket but had no tie. They clutched mugs of mulled wine.

"Yes," said Russell. "I've been to several other parks and we are by far the best."

"Yes," said the British woman, "we—" She stopped speaking. Mark was curious about why the woman had censored herself.

"Go on," said Russell.

"Oh, we love this park, we've been coming to South Africa for decades, and we've been to so many of them. All my jewelry is local. Can't wear it in the cities anymore. The only safe place is in the wild. Rather sad comment."

"You've been here before, to this park?" Stefanie asked.

The woman turned and smiled. Maroon lipstick was smudged across her teeth. "Yes, in fact we have. We were here two years ago, and it was quite an adventure. Very much like this time, actually. Seems last time there was trouble between cheetah cubs and lions as well."

"Julia," said her husband.

But Julia continued. "Almost like a radio play, with the CBs going off all the time, and in the dark you can imagine what is taking place out there. Anything is possible in the dark."

"It *is* very dramatic," said Russell. "Excuse me." He stepped away to talk to another guest.

Mark swallowed the last of his wine. He caught Stefanie's eye, held up his mug, and slipped away. While he was waiting for the mulled wine, he noticed Aaron talking to the young man from the main lodge, the one he'd encountered while looking for the bathroom during the group dinner. Aaron handed the man a mug of wine. Mark stepped out of line, left the boma, and paused for a moment to determine where he was. The air was cooler away from the fire, and Mark thought he should have worn a heavier sweater. He corrected himself. In South Africa it was a *jersey*. It was darker outside the boma, but Mark's only fear was of a staff member stopping him and asking what he was doing. He wasn't sure yet himself.

The road was groomed and easy to walk on, and Mark arrived at the main lodge in a few minutes. There were lights on deeper inside the building. The last game drives of the evening had ended less than an hour before. Mark entered, walked down the hallway, found the bathroom, and relieved himself. Then he went directly to the office he'd seen. The door was slightly ajar and Mark knocked. No answer. He knocked again. Still no answer. Mark slowly opened the door, and saw that nobody was at the controls. He entered and sat down.

The equipment seemed related to the CB system. It was the dispatch center and helped keep the various Land Rovers informed about where in the park each was going and what animals they were after. The computer was on, and its screen saver was a group photograph of a soccer team wearing green and yellow uniforms. When Mark touched the space bar the image vanished and a map of the park appeared. It showed the location of the animal habitats, the guests' glass cabins, the main lodge, and the boma. Each building had a camera icon next to it, and when Mark clicked on a glass cabin, a live video stream appeared on screen. A camera was obviously affixed to a nearby tree. The guest had left a lamp on and the whole room was visible. Chair, dresser, couch, bed. Mark stared, and then closed the image.

The primary map showed clusters of small blue, green, red, orange, and yellow dots. Mark used the mouse to hover over one of the red dots, and the word "olifant" popped up with what looked like GPS coordinates. When he moved the mouse to a yellow dot, the word "leeu" appeared, along with the numbers. The other dots indicated the precise locations of the other animals. They must have been tagged with chips that tracked their locations.

On the far side of the screen there was a row of the same colored lights, each paired with an audio icon. Mark clicked on the yellow audio icon, and nothing happened. He clicked it again. Nothing. He was about to quit, but pulled the mouse across the map again. Dozens of small audio icons on the map lit up and he understood these were the speakers like the one he'd seen in the tree outside his glass cabin. They were scattered all throughout the park, even in the forests and the savannah. An icon showed there was a speaker near the main lodge, the building where Mark sat. He clicked it, and the sound of a lion roaring startled him. It was loud, as though the lion was right outside. He clicked it again, and the lion roared again. Mark wondered whether it was audible at the boma, and had an idea. The boma was clearly marked on the map, and when he clicked on it, he heard the sound of a lion roaring further in the distance. For him to hear it inside meant it was very loud at the boma. He pictured the other guests, half-drunk, suddenly quiet and still. This was more fun than seeing lions in person. He hit the icon again, and heard the roar filter in through the building's walls.

He remembered the young man who was supposed to be operating the controls. Surely he would return once he heard the sound. Mark stood, walked to the door, and glanced down both hallways. Nobody was there, so he sat down again and clicked the icon several more times, pausing to listen to the faint roar coming from the boma.

That's good enough, he thought. But instead of leaving he clicked on one of the other lodges. Inside, lit by a bedside lamp, Dr. Hoost lay flat on his back while a naked woman straddled him. Mark recognized her as a server at the feast a couple days before. She had smiled at him. Several minutes passed while Mark watched with mild interest. His mind wandered to the Zulu dancer he'd seen change clothes at the Valley of a Thousand Hills.

"You are in trouble," a voice said. Mark turned and saw Aaron. He held his machine gun, no doubt for the walk from the boma to the main lodge in case there really had been a lion.

"Actually no," Mark said. "*You're* in trouble. This is pathetic."

Mark watched Aaron's face. It softened.

"Don't," Aaron said. "Please."

"You're ripping off tourists. Not to mention watching their cabins."

Aaron gestured in the direction of the boma. "They're having fun. They don't know any better."

"I want my money back."

"You seem to be enjoying Dr. Hoost's good fortune."

Mark started to respond, but then wondered what would become of Stefanie's professional relationship with Dr. Hoost if everyone learned about the tryst.

Russell walked down the hall and joined Aaron, barely acknowledging Mark. "Everyone is holding tight at the boma. They are frightened but happy. They think the lions are right outside." He laughed, and added, "If they live through this they'll have the best story to tell their neighbors."

"It was Mark," said Aaron.

"I can see that," said Russell. He turned to Mark. "Your wife is hysterical. She thinks you've been eaten by a lion."

Mark smiled despite himself, but said, "Your park is a fraud."

Russell glanced at Aaron, and then said, "I can arrange for your money back. And would you like a complimentary week watching mountain gorillas? I have a friend who guides in Uganda. Owes me a favor."

"Is that fake too?" Mark asked.

"*This* isn't fake," Russell said. "It's management. It's how we provide the best experience possible for our guests. They wouldn't want it any other way."

"Unless they knew."

"Right," said Russell.

"Is every animal managed?"

"Big cats and elephants" said Aaron.

"And us. The people," said Mark, but even as he said it his anger diminished. He felt elated, energized. He saw himself as Russell and Aaron saw him, an ignorant visitor, a small piece of a routine which had long ago become dull for them. Mark was an opportunity for them to have a bit of fun, just as he'd been tempted to trick the second graders on field trips to his planetarium in Chicago.

"You won't tell the others?" asked Russell, who must have noticed the softening of Mark's brow and jaw.

"Bastards."

"Good," said Aaron. "I need this job."

Russell patted Mark on the shoulder. They walked back to the boma, while Mark thought how little the lies mattered.

It was people's perception that counted, the stories they built around the raw details of their trip to Africa. To ensure their peace of mind was a good thing, a kind of honor, like a parent tucking a small child into bed saying there was nothing to fear in the dark because God would protect them.

* * *

As Mark and Stefanie packed for their trip home her relief turned sour.

"You could have been killed!"

"No, I couldn't."

"You heard the lions!"

"It wasn't real."

"Don't start that again."

Mark explained some of what he'd found in the main lodge, and how it was he who'd made the lion echo across the park. He was telling her about their refund and the Ugandan mountain gorillas when she exploded.

"Asshole!" She threw a dirty sock and Mark ducked. "Everyone was afraid. You think you can just toy with people like that? People who care about you? Me?"

Mark picked up the sock. "*Everyone* was scared? Even that old British couple?"

"What does that matter? Yes!"

Mark smiled.

"You're happy?"

"I am."

He didn't dare tell Stefanie about the video cameras and how they were positioned to see through their cabin walls.

* * *

It was dark but dawn was approaching early next morning when they began their final game drive. Russell, Aaron, Mark, and Stefanie were silent as they rumbled across the savannah.

"Why is everyone so glum?" asked Dr. Hoost. He was grinning. Nobody had told him the truth about the lions they'd heard the night before, or the speakers hidden in the landscape, or the GPS system, or the video cameras. Mark had settled into the idea his fees would be refunded and, if he could convince Stefanie, there was the prospect of a free trip to Uganda to look at gorillas. Telling Dr. Hoost would only complicate things.

"Last day, I guess," said Mark.

Stefanie glared at her husband.

"The cheetah pups might be up ahead," Russell said over his shoulder. He had to pretend, for Dr. Hoost's sake.

Aaron told a story about what had happened overnight. The lion they'd heard near the boma during the bonfire had strayed from the cheetah pups. Either he'd killed them all and moved on by the time the group heard him, or he'd driven them deep into hiding. Now the guide and the tracker were taking the tourists to where the pups were thought to be. Mark glanced at Stefanie while Aaron spoke. She was livid.

"Enough!" She shouted. None of them had ever raised their voice on a game drive and Russell stopped the vehicle. Everyone looked at Stefanie. Mark felt the muscles in the back of his neck contract. "I've had enough of this bullshit about the cheetah pups," Stefanie said. "I never want to see a cheetah pup again. I hope to God I never hear another lion roar."

Dr. Hoost reached back and touched Stefanie's shoulder. "Are you okay?"

The dawn had come and the sun would soon rise. Mark ignored his wife and noticed the field of tall yellow grass was swaying. The wind had picked up even in the last few minutes. In the distance, for the first time, he noticed the telephone lines that indicated the highway and the edge of the game reserve. He looked at Stefanie, expecting her to tell the whole story to Dr. Hoost and end the farce. But she ignored her colleague's question.

"Take us to see the aardvark," she said to Aaron. "We need to see the aardvark one more time before we go back to Chicago. If you can find it."

Russell and Aaron looked at each other. Neither spoke.

"I agree," said Mark. "Take us to the aardvark." Stefanie would never accept that mystery, trickery, and deception were always hiding behind the appearance of order. She was stuck in the banal world of bodies, of wounds, of pain, but also of healing.

Dr. Hoost was silent as Russell started the engine and turned the Land Rover around. They drove for an hour, passing zebra, water buffalo, wildebeest, and an elephant before Russell slowed the vehicle and Aaron whispered they were approaching a place an aardvark may have a burrow. It was off the road and the creature had likely bedded down for the day, but they would try to find it.

Stefanie stood on the back seat of the Land Rover, put her hand on its railing, and hopped onto the dirt road. "This way?" she asked, and before Aaron could stop her, she walked into the thick scrub brush and was gone.

Mark leapt out of the Land Rover but Russell and Aaron both yelled for him to stop. Aaron unlocked the rifle from its compartment in the front seat and walked into the brush. The sun was up but the shadows were long and Mark couldn't see where the two had gone.

"This happens more often than you'd think," Russell said. He was unconcerned. "Don't worry. Aaron will bring her back."

"Which anti-malaria drug is she taking?" Dr. Hoost asked Mark.

"We're not taking anything," Mark said.

"Some have horrible side effects," Dr. Hoost said.

Leaves rustled in the brush and Stefanie stepped back into the road. She was waving the camera and smiling. "I think I found its burrow," she said. "But I couldn't see any animals inside." Russell ignored her. "Where's Aaron?"

"I don't know. I heard him coming, but then I thought he turned back."

"Get back in," Russell said to Stefanie and Mark, "and wait for me."

He stepped into the bush and the sound of his movements through the shrubbery soon faded. A minute later he screamed.

"Dr. Hoost! Dr. Hoost!"

The doctor turned his face toward the woods.

"Dr. Hoost, under my seat, the antivenom kit, bring it. Everyone follow my voice, we need to carry Aaron out of here. He's bitten by a mamba."

Mark, Stefanie, and Dr. Hoost sat still and looked at each other. The doctors left the truck, and Mark followed as they crashed through the brush, trailing the sounds of Russell's voice until they found Aaron lying on the ground. Dr. Hoost injected Aaron with anti-venom. He was conscious, but his breathing was slow and shallow. The puncture marks from the snake's fangs were plainly visible on Aaron's neck and left cheek.

Russell and Mark grabbed hold of Aaron's shoulders, while Stefanie and Dr. Hoost held his feet. They scurried through the trees and bushes back to the Land Rover, where they lay Aaron across the back seat. "We have a full clinic at the camp," Russell said, "but it's nearly an hour away on these trails."

The Land Rover jostled Aaron as they rambled. Dr. Hoost sat beside him on a small wedge of the back seat and made sure he didn't roll onto the floor. Over the din of the engine he and Stefanie shouted their medical options, but with the anti-venom already administered there was nothing more to do apart from checking Aaron's pulse and monitoring his labored breathing. Forty minutes later, Dr. Hoost yelled for Russell to stop. Then he said, "I'm sorry. He's gone."

Mark looked at Aaron and couldn't believe the man had died. His face was still sweating. His brown eyes were open. His hand still clasped Dr. Hoost's. Stefanie's face had turned pale green. Mark knew she'd had patients die before. Every doctor had. But this was different. She had lost her temper and rushed into the woods. If not for that, Aaron would still be alive. Somehow the thought of it gave Mark a sense of calm.

Afterward it didn't seem right to leave the game reserve so quickly, but Mark and Stefanie had hotel reservations and a series of flights to catch, and Dr. Hoost was on call at his hospital. As they changed into their travel clothes in their glass lodge, Mark tried to comfort his wife.

"It was his time, that's all," Mark said. He had finished changing and was reclined on their couch eating a banana.

Stefanie looked at him. Her eyes were dull. She said nothing.

"I'm sorry for his family," Mark said, "but think of it this way. The world is overpopulated. In the bigger scheme of things—"

"Enough!"

Mark stopped talking and thought about how his words must have sounded to his wife, a woman who had dedicated her life to helping others. Now she was staring at him, and her face paled and took on the green hue he'd noticed in the Land Rover after Aaron died.

"Who are you?" Stefanie asked.

* * *

Late that evening Mark and Stefanie were back in Durban drinking red wine in silence on the club level of their hotel. Their trip to the game park, and indeed the entire trip to South Africa, had gone too quickly for Mark. It seemed impossible he'd seen a man die from snakebite that very morning. Now, on the top floor of the hotel, with a view of city lights out one window and the dark Indian Ocean out the other, South Africa didn't seem so frightening.

They were sitting on a leather couch and Mark was flipping through the images in his camera when a female voice asked, "more wine?"

Stefanie nodded. Mark looked up and saw the woman from the Zulu village a week before. She seemed startled, and held the bottle poised above Stefanie's glass but didn't pour.

Mark said, "You're from the Zulu village." It felt like years ago.

"Yes." She was wearing the pale yellow blouse, beige skirt, and blood red shoes Mark had seen her remove in the entrance to the grass hut. "My other job."

Mark looked at the wine bottle, at the camera, and at his wife. Stefanie had venom in her gaze.

"I have a picture of you," he said to the woman.

"I'm sure you do," she answered, and gestured at the camera. "Did you see any wildlife?"

Liver and Onions

Diane Lefer

Ryan "R.C." Bowden left Elmira, N.Y. on his favorite day of the year—the day the coats come off, when women show their shapes and some skin. This was shortly before *Mon Cher Alphonse* closed its doors for good and three days after he took the bus to Corning to see Elisabeth's father where, after an alarming allergy attack in the man's office ("What did you spray on those plants!?!?") and proclaiming he could not be bought, he allowed as how he'd always wanted to try his luck in L.A.

A month later in Los Angeles, charged with murder, his court-appointed lawyer withdrew after he touched her "inappropriately" and he then asked his second public defender to get him an astrologer and a psychic. The lawyer was more concerned with the alibi witnesses: Rosa García, diagnosed with Alzheimer's; Marisa Hagopian, cogent but unlikely to be favorably disposed.

Rudy and I were interviewed by detectives as well as by the A.D.A. and the defense. We knew R.C. That's why I can't let it go.

* * *

"It was a false spring," Elisabeth said later. "The dogwood and wisteria froze. The coats went back on."

Same here in L.A. where the air early in April smelled like spring but felt damp and cold like fall.

Now, on these glorious days in May, I keep going back to the house in Van Nuys where R.C. lived briefly with Shannon Wozniak, Marisa, and Cody Steele (who considered him un-exceptional: "your typical frat boy, all about getting drunk and getting laid"). Where Elisabeth Miller has been staying, sleeping on the couch, since she flew out after hearing of the arrest on TV. I tell Rudy I'm going to visit Rosa, which is true.

When she shuffles to the door, crying out for Ryan, I say "It's me. Cati."

"Go away," she says, and so I do, and I go straight to the house next door. Where Ryan—R.C.—lived.

* * *

In this household, Shannon does temp work. Sometimes the phone rings with an assignment; mostly, it doesn't. She and Cody go to the occasional audition. They go to the health club—"That's where you make connections," says Cody, though he also says he's had better luck at A.A.

I don't know what they live on.

"It was Wednesday," says Marisa. But she's mostly at home or at the library working on her dissertation. Without classes or an office to go to on a schedule, it has to be easy for her to lose track.

"It could have been Tuesday," says Elisabeth. The others don't like her but she's paying a share of the rent without even being asked.

"He's the kind of damaged person," says Marisa, "who damages anyone who's close to him."

"Unless," says Elisabeth, smug, "you know to take care of yourself."

Marisa tugs at her braid and I sit there, listening, thinking how strange it is that R.C. is at the center of their consciousness and lives while it's becoming more and more clear that he has no center of his own. It's also strange that I don't want my husband to know I'm here. It's not that he'd disapprove. He never does.

I keep a lot from Rudy lately so I don't have to be confronted with his tolerance. He doesn't know I've visited R.C. in jail.

I sit across from him. It's magnetic. Not that I feel an attraction to *him.* It's more that in his presence a disconnected piece of me stirs, pulls closer, closer till I can almost believe it will snap into place.

There's something about being big, tall, and good looking that makes a man think he was born to a special destiny.

The way R.C. sees it, everyone benefited. No one got hurt.

"How's Rosa?" he says, like he cares, and maybe he does. "She's a nice lady." Rosa has fired another home health aide: "She looked like a nurse. People were going to think there's something wrong with me."

But it's easier to say, "Rosa's fine."

* * *

Mitigate: to make less severe, less painful. Less hostile. But in my work, this only refers to asking the judge to go easy on punishment.

If I were writing a mitigation report—which I am not; he is not a client of our firm—it might start off something like this:

CURRENT OFFENSES:

stalking, murder in the first degree with special circumstances.

SOCIAL HISTORY: Defendant was born in 1981. His parents, Joseph and Paulette, agricultural workers in New York State's Southern Tier (bordering Pennsylvania) were among the poor, rural population derisively referred to as "apple scabs" (after a type of orchard blight; no reference to non-union labor). According to his mother, they were repeat-edly told throughout their public school years that formal edu-cation for "apple scabs" was an unnecessary waste of time and taxpayer dollars. She (unlike her husband) did complete high school. The graduating class was recognized with a special field trip to Albany where they were introduced for the first time to elevators and escalators—this, mind you, in 1972. At the time, she was already pregnant as the result of rape which took place while employed during the pear harvest at a local or-chard. She gave the baby up for adoption.

* * *

I'm not working from depositions under oath or affidavits by the way. Just conversations. Joseph, dying in the prison hospi-tal, was not available to talk. I rely on Paulette for his story. He is illiterate, she told me on the phone. (Though I called several times we only had one real conversation. Usually one of the kids answered and said she wasn't feeling well, or she answered, too drunk to make much sense.)

Joseph enlisted or was drafted into the Army and served in Vietnam, returning to the Southern Tier region in 1975. After a period of drifting and short-term employment marked by sig-nificant alcohol and drug abuse (for which he served his first prison term), he reconnected with Paulette when they met at a local tavern. By then, 1980, seasonal orchard work was mostly in the hands of immigrant Jamaican labor and Paulette had found employment on the cleaning crew at the state hospital for the criminally insane, a job she was anxious to leave as the ammonia fumes set off asthma attacks. They married soon after she became pregnant and named the baby after the actor, Ryan O'Neal. The boy always preferred to go by the initials, R.C.

The marriage was a volatile one but five more children were born. "We couldn't afford them," according to Paulette, but her husband's alcoholism, having rendered him impotent most of the time, she'd stopped bothering with contraception. Did she consider abortion? "I don't think you could get one where we lived."

Paulette chooses to stay home rather than visit her son in jail or attend his trial—if you can call it choice when she has no money to make the trip and has children to care for, if you can call it care.

R.C. became the man of the house whenever his father was in jail, mostly short stretches, until the conviction for armed robbery in 2000 sent him to the state penitentiary in Elmira where he will almost undoubtedly die. They'd been renting in an unincorporated area when Joseph got the idea they needed to buy the place. Oil companies were exploring for gas. Property-owners were negotiating leases and royalties. All a man needed was capital, and so he got drunk and took his shotgun to the Mobil station.

That's when Paulette moved to Elmira with the kids so they could see him in prison on visiting weekends. "Elmira has a bad reputation in some quarters because of us," says Paulette. "Prisoner families. White trash."

The marriage was most amicable whenever Joseph was locked up. When he was home, he beat Paulette often and called her "savage" and "squaw." (Paulette denies being of Mohawk ancestry but R.C. did apply for college scholarships and admissions on diversity grounds and was angered when told he did not qualify.) Paulette defends her husband, citing his frustrations. "He couldn't read or write and they passed him grade to grade till it came time to graduate high school and then they wouldn't let him." As for her son, "He got the G.E.D., not the Regents"—the full academic diploma.

The family of seven lived in a two-room rental steps from the malodorous Chemung River. Paulette took to burning scented candles in the house. Everyone coughed from mold and mildew. The children were bitten by rats—this in R.C.'s account and Paulette's. Elisabeth, though she only saw the place from the outside, concurs it was "an awful depressing dump."

* * *

If I were writing a mitigation report for myself, I'd say *It was an accident. She didn't mean it.*

Mitigation is a growth industry here in California where the word "zealous" is an understatement when it comes to prosecutors. They love the death penalty. They love life without the possibility of parole though they sometimes must settle for an indeterminate life sentence of 45 years to life; 60 years to life; 85 years to life. Defendants will pay anything hoping to win some sympathy. The more I fail, the more work I seem to get. Extreme sentences just make other defendants more desperate.

"He deserves what he gets," says my husband even though what R.C. gets may be a lethal injection and this from a man who I thought opposed capital punishment.

"Rudy, think where he comes from. His father is in prison dying of cirrhosis. His mother is home drinking herself to death."

"Boo hoo," said Rudy.

"Doesn't it bother you the real killer may still be out there?"

Where Rudy comes from: Guatemala, where he survived a brutal dictatorship and mass murder. His history made my own distress seem trivial and at first I liked that. Now I think Rudy just gave up. Nothing bothers him because he has no faith that things can get better. That a person can change.

"R.C.'s the oldest child," I said. "The other kids expect him to save them. He didn't even know how to save himself."

"I won't insult animals by calling him one."

My husband is a surgeon humbly calling himself a mere mechanic who works on people instead of cars. Now this begins to seem like false modesty. He's like all the others, playing God, thinking he who saves lives is also entitled to take them.

But I've been getting used to it, the way the most gentle of men rage against any member of their gender who kills a woman, as if they all had something to prove.

And I'm getting used to the way the new generation of women—"girls"—is willing to sit around for hours talking about men. Why not? Think tanks and institutes employ some of the best minds of the nation to sit around studying the enemy. But why, I want to know, why aren't we talking about rightwing broadcasters and *their* lies? Is that too obvious? What about the BP oil disaster in the Gulf? Why aren't we talking about coal mine operators with no respect for human life? Why aren't we looking *out there?*

"Why aren't we talking about my $120,000 in student loan debt?" says Marisa.

"You should have moved to a civilized country where education is free," says Elisabeth.

I ask Cody for a refresher on the Serenity Prayer—the things we can change, the things we can't, "the wisdom to know the difference."

Then I listen as they talk about R.C.

"What can you possibly say about a man who always calls when the charge is so low on his phone, you have to strain to make out what he's saying?" And the background sounds: the rush and echo in the bowl, the diving splash, a couple of pings, the roar when he flushed, the son-of-a-bitch, this was on purpose, Elisabeth thought. It had to be. "He wanted me to picture him, phone in one hand, cock in the other."

But she merely finds this amusing. Smalltown life must have bored her half to death. She is so young: Elisabeth with her blood red lipstick, the Thomas the Tank Engine lunchbox she carries as a handbag, the ruby stud in her nose that looks more like the blood of a popped pimple than a jewel. Maybe R.C.

was an accessory, too. But to her credit, she's loyal. She paid for the astrologer and a psychic. She wanted to pay his bail but it was set at $2 million and they didn't want a trust fund; they wanted real estate. She said at first she'd stay for the trial. I told her I'd be surprised if it began before next year. "You mean he stays in jail till then?" So much for a speedy trial. (Why don't we talk about *that*?)

Elisabeth doesn't think he did it. "Our last night together? I called him names. I hit him. He never hit me. Never even raised his voice. I never saw the slightest hint of violence."

I don't think he did it either.

"He's a pathological liar," said Elisabeth. "He's a con man. He's not a killer."

"But Dewi was going to expose him. That could have been the stressor," said Shannon. She's apparently watched too many episodes of *Criminal Minds*.

"He came close to killing Shannon," said Marisa.

* * *

The only one who's dead is Dewi DeLanda. Sympathy for the accused doesn't mean I'm ignoring the victim. Dewi: the new face of America where the most exotic features now represent the girl next door. Willowy, soulful, racially ambiguous. Star quality, they said. She wasn't one of those indie film actresses with character in her face instead of beauty. Her skin, they said. Her luminous skin. In a city where women in the industry are joined at the hip with their makeup artists, there to fix the face any time a camera appears, Dewi had the glow, she had that skin in real life. And a voice like cream poured from a pitcher, rich, sensuous, wholesome. Dewi DeLanda was strangled in the parking lot of the Brentwood Country Mart the night of Tuesday, April 20. The news reports called her "an aspiring actress" much to Shannon's displeasure: "She had small roles in major motion pictures. She was recurring on a primetime series. If she was *aspiring*, what does that make me?"

Everyone should aspire. I do, though too often I'm not sure to what. R.C. aspired to escape the circumstances that could have defined him. He aspired to be who he wasn't and so the "girls" try to figure out who he is. I listen.

According to Elisabeth and his mother, during his brief attendance at community college, R.C. enrolled for a degree in criminal justice, not as surprising a choice as you might think given that prisons are the main provider of stable employment in the region.

He told Marisa he had a degree in psychology.

He told Shannon he'd studied at the Culinary Institute and was the chef at *Mon Cher Alphonse*.

"Waiter," said Elisabeth. With the restaurant closing, he feared he'd have to return to his old job, collecting the carcasses of dead horses and cattle, bringing them to the plant where the bodies were rendered, turned to tallow and hide.

In L.A., he became, first, a person of interest. An obvious suspect. He kept changing the story he gave the police.

"Yeah," said Elisabeth, "he lies. He'll convince you Monday is Tuesday and black is white, just for the hell of it. Just to show he can."

Now he's the defendant.

There's no physical evidence he killed her. No eyewitness. It's all circumstantial. And in spite of what R.C. claimed, it's unlikely they even met.

Talk talk talk. Shannon finds out Marisa had sex with him twice.

"He told me—" Marisa began. "Oh the hell with it. Never mind what he told me." She wears a single braid over her shoulder the way my little sister did. Meredith chewed on the end of hers when watching TV, till our mother cut her hair short to stop her. Marisa tugs hers when concentrating or, as now, put on the spot.

"He's a rat," said Shannon.

"They get a bad rap," said Marisa. She's getting a Ph.D. in animal behavior and ethology and ought to know. She told us about an experiment. To get food, the rat had to press a lever that gave the rat in the next cage a painful shock. The rats went hungry rather than hurt another rat which suggests that rats are more ethical, more empathic, than people.

When I repeated this to Rudy, he said, "The rat in the experiment might have been a particularly moral rat. It doesn't tell you much about rats in general. Most men don't kill. That one did." He kissed the top of my head in a patronizing way, but at least he was willing to see rats as individuals.

I see R.C. as a little boy with both parents drunks. A world of blackouts, missing hours and days, excuses, stories, lies. Is it possible a child can grow up never knowing there's such a thing as truth? His lies not premeditated, but rather a creative ability to improvise, filling in the blanks with whatever comes to mind. Words don't have the same weight to him as for me.

"Even if he did it," said Elisabeth, "I'm sure he doesn't feel guilty. Doesn't that mean he's not guilty? If he doesn't know right from wrong?"

If you don't think you're guilty, the only outcome of punishment is rage.

If you do think you're guilty, punishment can't be escaped, only deferred. So a person might conceivably live with only one foot in her own life, uncertain, and waiting.

In the county jail, they've taken away his earrings. They've put him in a jumpsuit. The glass separating us is dirty. I see him through a blur and I smell prison disinfectant and men's sweat, the oxymoronic and inescapable odor: antiseptic filth.

If you live with no consciousness of what you've done, if you're missing that part of your past, how can you be accountable?

Without your past, have you even got a self? What do you do with someone who's a figment of his own imagination?

"Are you all right in here?" I ask. "Are you safe?"

"I'm Mohawk," he says. "No one's gonna mess with me."

As though self-invention is self-defense. Survival. Sometimes something you don't know is dangerous turns out to be. And me, I can't stop staring at his hand, his strong fingers around the neck of the phone.

"How's Rosa," he says. "Everyone else was just after their pound of flesh."

"What do you think I'm after?" I say.

He smirks. "Rudy's a lot older than you."

"I am not asking anything from you," I say. "No pound of flesh." I think of Rosa, holding his pillow and breathing his scent, *mijo*. "It might do you good to know not everyone wants your body."

"The State of California wants my body. The State of California wants to tell my body when to stand up and when to lie down. When to eat. When to shower. When to shit.

"Why are you here?" he says.

* * *

Which is the same question Marisa asks.

"I was visiting Rosa and I thought I'd stop by."

(Rosa's niece has asked the agency to send a "hunk," but for now, Milagros is on the job and taking Rosa's abuse. She serves us coffee.

"I never believed the lies," says Rosa as she pours sugar onto the table.

"The sugar, Rosa," I say.

"Yes, I take two," she says and pours more. "You didn't believe either, did you?"

"That he killed her?"

"Millions. They said he killed millions." She is agitated until Milagros hands her a rag doll. She is serene as she rocks it and whispers, "A good man. A great man, *mijo*" and I realize she's not thinking of Ryan Collins Bowden but—oh my God—of Stalin.)

"My God, but you girls need Al-Anon," says Cody. "Co-dependent! Someone needs to tell you you're not supposed to figure *him* out. You're supposed to work on *yourself*."

"That's what I'm doing," says Shannon. "How can I work on myself if I can't figure out what happened to me with *him*? Before I moved out here," she says, "I called an old friend. She said she'd introduce me to single men. What were my criteria? Easy, I said. No substance abuse, no one who's racist or homophobic."

"And he should prefer having sex to watching TV," says Marisa.

"My *friend* says, 'I understand why you feel that way, but you realize how much you're limiting yourself.'"

We all laugh.

"So what happens?" says Shannon. "I end up sleeping with a murderer."

"We don't know that," Elisabeth says.

"At least he wasn't homophobic," says Cody.

"Oh my God," says Shannon. "You too—?"

"No," says Cody.

"Or racist," says Elisabeth. "Though you'd expect him to be. He could have been a skinhead or white supremacist. I always gave him credit because he isn't."

* * *

According to Cody, men like stupid women.

"And stupid men?" asks Shannon.

His tongue plays briefly on his lips. "Among other qualities."

According to my daughter, women like bad men. Kira's ideal is House, the pathological doctor on TV.

She is so young. I don't want her to be like Elisabeth, young enough to believe that taking a sick relationship in stride proves how strong, adult, and independent she is. The more trouble R.C. gives her, the more she's impressed with herself. Elizabeth was engaged to marry an MBA candidate at Cornell—until she met R.C.

"House is not good relationship material," I tell Kira.

She echoes me. "*Relationship material?* Mom, you don't talk like that. And you like the bad boys."

"Your father?" I say. "Anyway, *like* isn't the word or the emotion," and she gives me a look, something like superiority or contempt, like the look R.C. must have seen on Shannon's face sometimes, and I remember holding baby Kira in my arms thinking it's only natural she'll grow up to be a teenage girl who hates me.

"What about you?" says Marisa and I'm startled to be asked.

"I'm married." The words sound strange. If you asked, *Who are you?* I would say *I'm Cati,* not *I'm married,* and now I wonder if I'm about to be envied for this random status, or dismissed.

"Why am I single? I had sex with him," says Marisa. "Doesn't that count as stupid?"

"You seem superior even when you don't mean to," says Cody. "And you, Shannon—you're wearing a nurse's cap."

"Nurses don't wear caps anymore."

"Metaphorically. Anyone can see you're fucked up that way—ready to take care of people."

That *was* how they met. At the pool, both staying in temporary housing at Oakwood. Shannon in bikini, R.C., as always, a hunk. Not much swimming that day. Lots of splashing and drinking. R.C. walked her to her room, took her in his arms.

"I thought, like, *Wow!*" she says. "Then this other girl shows up. Drop-dead gorgeous, and R.C. suddenly says he doesn't feel well." Shannon thought it was bullshit when he turned, walked away, left her at the door. When he collapsed to the ground, of course she felt guilty.

It was Shannon who knelt over him and called 911, screaming about cardiac arrest and asking herself why the hell she'd never learned CPR. She pulled on some clothes and went along to the emergency room. "They wouldn't admit him, I figured because he doesn't have insurance." The real nurse told her R.C. was just drunk, she should take him home and let him sleep it off. "But even if he was drunk, people can go into a coma. He could die." Shannon tucked him into her own bed and sat up beside him all night, watching and listening to his every breath.

R.C. opened his eyes once, complaining of headache. She gave him an aspirin. She missed an audition, sitting beside him until he woke again late in the afternoon. He didn't remember a thing. According to Shannon, after she explained, he took her hand. "He says I saved his life and no one ever in all his years ever did for him as much as I did." When he complained again of headache, she offered the aspirin. "He freaked out and started yelling at me that he was allergic. So I told him I already gave him one. He says, 'I just thanked you for saving me when you could have fucking killed me!'"

"God," says Shannon. "It was just guilt upon guilt upon guilt."

A couple of weeks later, after they both moved into the house in Van Nuys, he came out of the bathroom one night with a pill in his hand, looking for bottled water.

"Wait!" Shannon tried to stop him. "What's that?"

"An aspirin."

"Don't!"

"What are you talking about?" he said, and swallowed it.

"Yeah, he's a pathological liar," said Elisabeth, with a shrug. "It's like he can't help it."

"It's called confabulation," said Cody. "You have blackouts. You have no idea what happened. You fill in the blanks and make it up. It's what we drunks do."

So there's a word for what I imagined.

Elisabeth sighed. "It's like he's doomed to inspiration."

* * *

She visits him in jail, too.

"What do you talk about?"

"I tell him I love him."

"Does he say he loves you?"

She answers, without hesitation, "He's under a lot of stress."

The most conventional lie of all, and he can't say it.

* * *

Rosa has her own idea about R.C.

"We were leafletting at Boeing. Or maybe it was Seal Beach? Vander … vander … Vanderberg." Her eyes dart. "They came and beat us. They beat him over and over. His head. They beat him over the head." Rosa and her alternate reality. Why on earth did I ask *her*? "I brought him home. You know he can't take care of himself."

* * *

"He told me he had a degree in psychology," said Marisa. "He said he was here to take a job in advertising. After years of running rats through mazes, he said he knew what made people tick."

If people are equivalent to rats and *if* you can flatten out and stereotype the rats, I think. But I don't object out loud. The larger question is why R.C. would tell lies when he was bound to be found out. It's not like they wouldn't notice soon enough he had no job. It's not like Marisa and Shannon weren't going to compare notes.

"All impulse," said Elizabeth. "He doesn't even realize when he's lying."

"Premeditation," said Marisa. "He figures the probabilities. It's statistical."

"And whose dissertation," asked Cody, "would be done if she could get the statistical chapter right?"

"The point is, does he get what he wants often enough? In spite of."

"I pitied him," said Shannon. "Then it became contempt. He must have sensed it." And when she fell apart—which she did—the sexual frustration was mixed with self-loathing, that she could be in thrall to someone she'd come to despise. "What kind of person lets herself fall that low?" she said. "I deserved what I got."

* * *

When I visit R.C., he's sometimes angry, mostly baffled. He, with his highly developed sense of honor which assures he's always ready to take offense.

What would it feel like to feel no guilt, no shame?

"Sociopath," says Rudy.

No wonder R.C. feels cheated: Sociopaths in this society usually do well.

He lies about everything.

I always told the truth—the factual truth—but never how I felt about the facts.

I'm trying to understand what I'm trying to say.

I'm trying to say what I'm trying to understand.

I'm trying to understand what I feel.

I feel okay, but coping is not as admirable as it might seem.

* * *

"I'm okay now," says Shannon. "Really. I'm really okay."

* * *

Elisabeth met him when her father took her to dinner at *Mon Cher Alphonse*. He thought it was great that a rundown town like Elmira had a fine French restaurant. All these people fleeing New York City moving into the gingerbread Victorians on the Near West Side. Most transplants don't take. *Mon Cher Alphonse* closed in less than a year.

The place stayed open long enough for R.C. to pass Elisabeth a note while her father had his head down signing the check.

"You don't want to know what it said," she says.

The night before R.C. left Elmira, the week before the restaurant closed its door for good, the waitstaff threw him a party. When Elisabeth showed up, he was back in the kitchen, pressed up against Wendy.

"It's how he is," Elisabeth says.

(On the phone, Wendy said, "He wanted to spend the night with me, but Elisabeth was driving him to the airport in the morning so he couldn't.")

"Why do you even care about him?" asked Marisa. "Your letters would come with lipstick kisses on the envelope."

"Don't," said Shannon.

"He'd mutter about the rich bitch and throw them out unread," said Marisa.

"So how come he was going to send for me once he got settled?"

"Or so he said."

"He phoned me at least once a day to say how much he missed me."

Elisabeth cried.

Marisa tugged her braid. "I'm sorry," she said. (Later she told me what she's really sorry about is sleeping with him, guilty that she hurt Shannon.) "It's a hard truth but I think you should know."

"It's not that," Elisabeth said, "It's just that I feel so sorry for him."

* * *

"Everyone benefited," Elisabeth said. "That's what he always said. I was lucky my parents couldn't stand him. If it hadn't been for R.C., I would've been caught up in the whole family thing, all the time. I would've been trapped."

The stories we tell ourselves.

"You were telling us about the party," Shannon said.

"The chef baked him a special cake. Hazelnut cream. He spat out the first mouthful. Said he was allergic to nuts. Of course he wasn't. Everyone felt terrible," she said.

* * *

I don't feel bad about Rosa. Rudy and I were *there* but it was the niece who told him he could stay. All Rosa lost was a few hundred dollars and she doesn't even know it.

Early in her life, Rosa rejected Jesus in favor of Marx, and even Stalin, but in '68, when she opened the Centro Aztlán, La Virgen de Guadalupe presided—to reassure parents that their children would not be corrupted, and anyway, Rosa still revered Guadalupe as a symbol of her identity, her race. Rudy and I have contributed to her youth center for years and met her once or twice at fundraisers. Then just this April, we were on the hunt one afternoon for the best handmade tortillas we could find. A strange day. We had to detour around where a Hazmat team was cleaning up a spill of what turned out to be Alfredo sauce. We pulled into the lot at a strip mall when we saw the words *hechas a mano* and the Guadalupe mural on the wall. There we spotted Rosa, older, hair undone, running her hand over the image.

I went to her. "I'm sure you don't remember me." If I'd had any idea, those are not the words I would have chosen.

Rosa stroked the Virgin. "She looks familiar. Do you know her?"

"Rosa," I said. "Can we drive you home?"

She told me she lived in Las Vegas. It was Rudy who had the idea to ask for her phone. He called the number on speed dial: "Niece."

The niece, Vanessa, gave us Rosa's address—in Van Nuys, not Las Vegas. "California pulled her drivers license. She thinks Nevada will give it back to her." She met us at the house. "She lives in her own reality. And every time I get her a home health aide, she fires her."

We never did get our tortillas. When R.C., duffel bag on his shoulder, came storming out of the house next door, Rosa noticed him first. "Look! Look!" she whispered. "Wow!" Then "Hello!"

He walked up the path, shaking himself like a wet dog. "They're filming porn in there. I won't put up with that crap."

"*Mijo*," said Rosa though as far as we know, Rosa never had children. "Come."

Vanessa asked for ID. They talked a while. Rosa did need someone. Inside, the place wasn't as bad as it seemed at first: what looked like piles of cockroach body parts turned out to be the hulls Rosa spat out while snacking on popcorn. The house didn't need much help, but she did.

Rosa showed R.C. to his room.

* * *

The only pornographic sight next door to Rosa had been R.C. walking around the house naked.

"The show-off!" said Cody.

He climbed into Shannon's bed but wouldn't make love. She paid the rent. R.C. said, "I can't be bought" (which is what he said to Elisabeth's dad before he took the $10,000 check).

The money he arrived with didn't last. He asked to borrow bus fare to go on job interviews, but he spent it on *Variety*, *People*, and *Us*. ("Maybe he's the normal one," said Elisabeth.) He turned the pages so quickly, Shannon thought he was speed-reading. Then she realized he just looked at the photos. Barely literate, she thought. How on earth did he get through community college?

"Professors took an interest in me."

Female professors, no doubt. She'd assumed he'd had affairs with them but more likely he just turned them on with the promise. He wasn't bought as long as he refused to deliver whatever it was he was being paid for.

As far as Shannon was concerned, the relationship should have been safe. She'd been in love before, she said. She'd been hurt. An arrangement was better. R.C. had free rent, steady sex. He was welcome to take advantage of her, she thought, since self-interest would keep him from hurting her.

"There's the flaw in your logic," said Marisa. "He's poor, right? Look how they vote. Self-interest?"

* * *

Why was it in his interest to stay in touch with Rudy and me? One night after he'd moved in with Rosa, he invited us to dinner. On our way over, my cell phone rang. "Could you pick up some parmesan." He called again asking for bread. We already had the wine. Rudy and I exchanged glances, but said nothing.

At the house, the parmesan went into the refrigerator. He shelved the wine and bread. We didn't say anything. We didn't understand. While Rudy kept Rosa occupied, I joined R.C. in the kitchen as he sautéed a pan of liver and onions. (Even Rudy couldn't eat it.)

I felt uneasy enough to lift the lid of the cookie jar where Vanessa had left $300 for emergencies. The jar was empty.

"I had an emergency," R.C. said. I stared at him. He stared back. He said, "You have beautiful breasts."

* * *

Which still doesn't explain why I can't let it go.

Shannon only thinks she has.

* * *

"Yeah, okay, I'm fucked up," Shannon said to Cody: "Doesn't that count as stupid?"

"No. You're still in control. You're not fragile. Men like damaged women."

"I'm as damaged and broken as anyone."

"The point isn't to *be* fragile. It's to *look* fragile."

I think Shannon does look fragile, like one of those tremulous victims you just want to slap.

"Look, I knew it wouldn't last," she said. She would've dumped him sooner or later. "But not yet!" Back at Oakwood, the sex was great—the passion, the urgency, but after a while you start to want some tenderness. R.C. wasn't capable of that. "At least not with me," she said, looking from Marisa to Elisabeth.

Marisa looked away. Elisabeth laughed. "Tenderness? No."

* * *

Rudy is capable of tenderness. But he has limits. I just don't know what they are. My husband left his country behind and never looked back. He cut all ties. That means he tolerates up to a point, but once the line is crossed, there's no turning back.

What is it that cannot, must not, be forgiven?

I'm sure something I do or don't do has to be too little or too much.

"Just tell me," I ask him. "Tell me."

* * *

"What do you want from me?" Shannon asked R.C. "What am I doing? Or not doing?" What made him want her, and then not?

After the first time they had sex, he said he'd get her onto the Fox lot. "He offered to show me Marilyn Monroe's dressing room." She knew it was bullshit, such a parody of L.A. bullshit she assumed he was joking. ("Though how did he know it was in Building 86?" Anyone who reads fan magazines and crap like *People* ...)

"He just wanted to do something nice for you," said Elisabeth. "And because he couldn't, he made it up."

When he asked for a ride to LAX to search for the luggage containing the only copy of the rough cut of his film, Shannon believed him.

The film was called *French Service*. It was a romantic comedy he'd written and directed and charged to five different credit cards. It starred, he said, Dewi DeLanda.

The airline denied knowledge of any missing luggage. R.C. didn't have a claim check. ("Of course not! They made me gate check it!") He was devastated more than angry. How would he break the news to Dewi? "We watched her on TV together," said Shannon.

How would he ever pay off the debt? The luggage, the film, were lost for good.

"How could you check something so valuable?" she wanted to know. "Why wasn't it in your carry-on?"

He looked so hapless. It's just the way men are, she thought, especially men as good looking as this one. They're used to everything going their way. They can't imagine anything can go wrong.

He took her hand. He ran his thumb over her knuckles. They stayed in bed for the next couple of days till the space opened up and Shannon moved into the house in Van Nuys. R.C. phoned her. Next thing she knew, she was inviting him to move in.

When Shannon finally asked him to get out of her bed and sleep on the couch (where Elisabeth still smells his scent in the cushions), "He's like all surprised. Like, *Why?* He looked at me like I'd betrayed him."

"I'm the one who got him to move out," said Cody. "I come in one night and he sits up and lets the sheet fall off his shoulder."

"Great shoulders," said Elisabeth.

"'Can I ask you something?' he says. 'When you go to an audition, don't you feel like a piece of meat?' I thought, that's it, he's got to go."

"But I'm the one who told him," said Shannon. "He packed and stormed out. But first he looked at me and said, 'I thought you were my friend.'"

* * *

What Shannon really feels guilty about is that she's the one who told R.C. about an interview in which Dewi DeLanda said she liked to shop at Diesel Books. The clerk there remembers a lot of people started coming in after the interview but R.C., he said, went further than most, coming in repeatedly, asking about Dewi, saying they had worked together. R.C. is also remembered at Frida's Tacos and Reddi Chick where he'd order food and sit for hours in the courtyard, watching, waiting.

"Dewi was uneasy about it," according to the bookstore clerk, "because she said she'd never heard of this guy or his film. She was a beautiful person, friendly, down-to-earth. I hope he gets the lethal injection."

* * *

I don't know what the words mean anymore: *guilty, not guilty.*
If I could be like R.C., words would be music, sound waves,
whatever sounds right at the time. (Sometimes it's just stupidity
like the time the court stenographer rendered *Amended Complaint* as *A man dead complaint.*) I think I know what *injustice*
is but I no longer know what people mean by *justice.*

I want things black and white and clear as much as the next
person.

* * *

But what you say ain't what you get.

* * *

"I love him," says Elisabeth. "That gives me clarity."

* * *

PERSONAL AND PSYCHOLOGICAL FACTORS
In evaluating the total life circumstances of this defendant, we
can say he's like a rat in a maze who's learned the fastest route
to the reward.

"He's not a metaphor," said Rudy. "He's a killer."

Accuracy before truth: "*Like* a rat," I said, "is a *simile.*"

* * *

In a city where Dewi DeLanda (as I've heard from Shannon)
performed for free at several small black-box theatres, her work
onstage is never mentioned in the nonstop TV coverage of her
death.

In a city where the ideal is to be perfectly odorless, R.C.,
who may or may not have killed her, used a balsam gel to spike
up his short black hair. He showered with Irish Spring, leaving
him so scented you could tell with your back turned or eyes
closed when he entered the room. Shannon is embarrassed to

admit (though obviously can't hide it) that she now uses the soap he left behind. "I don't want him back, but I still like to smell him on my skin."

Ironic. His model of reality doesn't pass the smell test.

Three earrings—one diamond stud and two small rings—in his right ear. "Right side, 'cause I'm straight." Maybe in Elmira. In L.A., is there any significance these days to which ear you pierce? Contact lenses. "I have to," he told Shannon, as though he had a particular disorder of the eye. But, "my eyebrows don't line up. When I wear glasses, whatever I do they look crooked." He arrived with several thousand dollars and three tuxedos. "Ready for the red carpet," he said. In Elmira, he owned one tux, needed for his job.

Elisabeth's father offered him the money to go away. "You do realize the relationship is unsuitable."

R.C. didn't get angry. Arrogant, maybe. He said, This is the U.S.A. in the 21st century, not some English novel." So he did learn something in school.

"You are a *waiter*," said the man.

"French service," R.C. said, with pride. Before leaving, he bought two more tuxedos and got a tattoo on his right bicep. Not what you'd expect: a little girl holding a flower.

We grow up with those songs: The man who can't offer riches gives his heart.

"The night he cooked dinner ... " Shannon rolls her eyes.

"The night I was making pasta," says Marisa, "he comes into the kitchen and covers the pot with the lid. I removed it. He looks at me in disbelief and says, 'Are you the one who's lived in Rome?' Not exactly a lie. He didn't exactly say he'd lived in Rome. He certainly implied it."

Tonight it's Cody who's making the pasta. "Are you staying for dinner?" he says. It isn't an invitation. I want to say I'm harmless, but I just hover, waiting to hear more.

"He was always talking about his French restaurant," says Shannon. "Then he cooked dinner for me one night. Liver and onions."

"Sweetbreads," says Elisabeth. "*Les rognons.*"

"No. Liver and onions. I mean he was really trying. I felt bad I just couldn't eat it.

* * *

"Mostly," Shannon said, "I was careful not to humiliate him."

"R.C.?" said Elisabeth. "He's been humiliated all his life."

* * *

To mitigate a sentence. To mitigate what amounts to nothing more or less than retribution. Revenge.

* * *

"You don't believe in change," I say to Rudy. "I can't accept that." My husband has no faith in governments or in people. And what have I managed to change? Nothing.

He tells me a good relationship is when you live with someone whose imperfections don't bother you too much.

But I don't want to be accepted. I want to be better.

"I chose the imperfections I'm willing to live with."

"Then you should have married someone like Elisabeth."

"Who?"

I've forgotten he doesn't know. Lately I find myself in places and situations and with people I don't tell him about. Not that I think I've done wrong. "Neither one of you really gives a damn."

And it doesn't even bother him that I said that, or that I've done things lately that could have turned out badly, acting on impulse. It all seemed to make sense, like the child who held her clothes against the electric heater until the flames burned down the house from which her sister failed to escape.

"It doesn't matter," he says and maybe means it. A lot of words are just words. A lot of promises are broken. Not everyone feels the same way about being lied to.

He says, "I love you, Cati." I don't even know what that means when the woman he says he loves is someone I don't care for.

"Something would have to bother you. Something would be too much." But how do you put into words something you haven't felt yet? "Just tell me."

All he says in return is *Cati*, my name.

* * *

"You don't tell us anything about *you*," says Shannon.

Elisabeth says, "You're like the person who stays sober when everyone else is wasted."

"Designated driver," I offer. I want to assure them I'm harmless.

"No. The bitch who watches and judges and silently laughs."

"Cody doesn't drink," I say.

"But he's got a problem. What's yours?"

* * *

Sometimes I think it's not guilt but lack of faith in the solidity of things.

* * *

THE TIME-LINE

Evening of Sunday, April 18: Felice confronts Shannon who confronts R.C.

Early morning hours of Monday, April 19: Shannon attempts suicide.

Tuesday, April 20: Murder of Dewi DeLanda. Marisa
confronts R.C.?
Wednesday, April 21: Or Marisa confronts R.C. now? Why
would she wait a day?

* * *

I was unable to track down "Felice," but here's Shannon, tran-
scribed from tape:

*This woman comes to the door. She asks my name and I
tell her. She says, "Good, now we can get a restraining order
against you." She says I've been stalking R.C. I tell her the
relationship is over and if she wants him, she's welcome to him.
She says, "Relationship? He doesn't even know your name."*

I tell her we lived together for weeks.

*"In your fantasy," she says. She tells me he's afraid of me. Me?
I saved his life. I show her photos on my cell phone.*

"PhotoShop," she says. "Are you taking your meds?"

*I push past her. She's grabbing at me screaming Restrain-
ing Order and R.C. comes into the entryway. He acts like he
doesn't even know me. Then he gets all kind and concerned.
He puts his arms around me. "Do something for me," he says.
I thought I'd already done plenty. "Get help," he says. "I don't
know who you are or what your mental health history is, but
you need help."*

*"Do you see the kind of person he is?" I say to Felice. "We
were living together. Some nights he didn't bother to come
home. I knew he was fucking around. I had to fight with him
to get him to use a condom. I hope you do. You don't know
where he's been."*

I say to her, "The one time he tried to do something nice, he took money from my purse and went out to buy food to cook me dinner. You know what he made? Liver and onions. Would you eat liver and onions?"

* * *

No. That, at least, I'm sure of.

* * *

It's a lie that no one got hurt.

Shannon stumbled back across the yard and driveway, back into the house. Sometime around the midnight hour, she stumbled into the bathroom just to look at her own face, and what she saw was two shellshocked eyes surrounded by blur. Being lied to, being lied to again and again is a form of torture. It tears the fabric until the world spins away from you, leaves you in empty space. The night flying past. The room tiltwise, the room dropping. Shannon was plunging, flying apart at the seams. She didn't hate him as much as she hated the desire she still felt for his body. Her palms against the mirror to steady herself, all she saw was him, R.C. standing right there, the only time she ever saw him *think*. He touched the soul patch beneath his lip, covering it with his hand, shave it or no? Then, her tears falling and to her horror those tears were as much about his pain as about her own.

I think she just needed to fix reality in place, to make the shifting stop.

She reached for the razor.

"I'm okay now," she says.

That night, Marisa found her.

* * *

I used to tell my story over and over again—the fire I started, my sister's death—till through the words, the repetition of fact, I became not *me*, but a bloodless representation of my life.

"I know you didn't do it," I say to R.C. "Please just tell me you feel bad about *something*."

"Bullshit!" He vibrates with self-righteous anger. I watch him walk away, a body of such husky grace and power, and I think of Shannon, of her disappointment, her shame and anger when he left her at the door only to collapse minutes later on the pavement. This time, he doesn't fall.

* * *

It's no lie that I do visit Rosa though she doesn't recognize me. So what? I just start talking. "Rosa, if a person has maybe once done something that can never be made right ... If it happened suddenly, inadvertently, but the result is just the same as if she did it on purpose ... Once a person knows she's capable, we're all capable, of so much damage, what happens to such a person's footing?" I think the world isn't solid then, when you can't know what your words or acts will do. And I think Rosa isn't listening. "It's too random," I say. "If we hadn't seen you and driven you home and just at that moment, R.C. was coming out the door ..."

"Ryan!" she cries. "Ryan! Ryan!" Milagros brings her the rag doll. She clutches it. She rocks and whispers. As long as she's holding the doll to her heart, Rosa is serene.

So is Marisa, her conscience untroubled. "I went next door to have it out with him. He says, 'What are you doing here? Aren't you supposed to be at yoga?' My yoga class was Wednesday night, so I said to him, no, today's Tuesday. He said, 'What do you mean? Today's Wednesday.'"

"That's what he does," says Elisabeth.

"So how can you be sure?" I say. "It could have been Tuesday."

"Wednesday," says Marisa. "Just like I told the police. I wasn't with him when Dewi was killed. I'm absolutely sure it was Wednesday."

The astrologer doesn't remember him which I don't believe—how many consultations does he do in jail with high-profile defendants?—but he allows as how Mercury may have been in retrograde.

The psychic won't repeat what she told him. Client confidentiality. "But do you want me to contact Dewi?" No! She held my wrist and both of us could feel my blood pulsing. "You want answers you're not going to find." Then she said, "Think of the maze as essential to amazement." She held out her palm for the fee.

* * *

We pay for this: The perilous consolation of words.

Conversations
with the Rest of the World

An Tran

The doctors came in droves when Lily was three. White coats who smelled in a way that pricked the inside of her nose with needles and who made her wear heavy uncomfortable blue aprons. They put her inside a tiny room with a one-eyed monster that revolved its head around hers while the ground hummed so deeply she felt her own stomach quake with it.

Later, sitting in her mother's lap, Lily watched one of the doctors move his lips the way her parents did. She read the lip patterns with a hot blade of envy rising in her chest, wondering what magic adults possessed that allowed them to understand each other. When Lily moved her lips in the same way, neither her mother nor father offered the slightest hint of recognition that Lily was understood. On the wall behind the doctor was a framed light that held a piece of black paper and a white glowing picture that looked like a small head with dark swirling shadows in the middle. After watching the doctor point at a whorl of gray on the picture and then Lily's ear, she understood that the picture was of Lily herself. The doctor's lips moved in a way she had never seen before, a new pattern and a new idea that she would come to know intimately. His lips stretched into an open line and she could see the tip of his tongue pressed to the roof of his mouth. When his tongue released, his upper teeth met his lower lip. The new word he spoke was one that would hinge onto Lily for her whole life; it was her identity: *deaf*.

* * *

At the age of four, Lily was introduced to a young, pretty woman named Miss Rachel. Miss Rachel had thick-framed rectangular glasses, blonde hair that was always tied back, and wore an assortment of colorful dresses with skirts that moved like thin curtains swaying in the wind.

On the first day, Miss Rachel handed Lily an apple and then took it away. She immediately started crying and Miss Rachel made a closed hand, pressing her index knuckle against her cheek, and pivoted her hand back and forth. At the same time, she mouthed the word Lily knew was *apple*—first an open and round mouth, next the lips met and a puff of air burst through to open the lips once more. Lily continued to weep and Miss Rachel showed her the apple this time. With her free hand, she performed the odd gesture again. And again. And again. Until Lily's tears had long stopped and she began to watch the ritual with curiosity, and then finally mimicked the movement herself. Miss Rachel clapped and smiled brightly and nodded with fervor as she handed Lily the apple. This time, she did not take it away. It took all week for Lily to understand that this gesture also meant *apple* and that her hands had the power to telegraph her thoughts.

Language came easily. Lily supplanted lip patterns she knew for these new signs and gestures. The new arrangement of words and ideas to transmit a thought fell into place with repetition and constant communication. And now Lily could not stop; she signed every moment as thoughts collided into and stacked atop each other. Thoughts multiplied into layers and bloomed an orchard in her mind. Her mother joined in on these lessons; for the first time, Lily could convey her thoughts, wants, frustrations with her. Admittedly, her mother was slow to pick up the nuances. She thought she could simply replace signs for words in English rather than learn the signs as a new language with its own grammar. Lily's father was notably absent during these sessions, exiling himself into the basement for stretches. Her mother occasionally rose and traveled down to the basement to chastise her father into keeping the noise of his guitars down, although she was the only one disturbed.

On one of her mother's trips into the basement, Miss Rachel explained to Lily how she was special. She had Lily place her small hands on her neck as she spoke. It vibrated in much the same way that Lily's did when she cried or screamed. And then Miss Rachel signed, The vibrations are sounds. Everything that can move can make a sound in some way. Most people's ears can sense the vibrations and make sense of them. This is called hearing.

It was magic to Lily. She was transfixed by the mysticism of it. People could sense things without looking. People could tell what direction it came from. How far away. Lily brimmed with ugly jealousy. Not because of the sense itself, but because people could communicate without looking. She couldn't imagine communicating with more than one person. When Lily signed to Miss Rachel, Miss Rachel became her whole world.

* * *

Every weekend, her father played his records and Lily positioned herself on the ground very near to the speakers. The sensations were thrilling—a magical confluence of vibrations, melding together in such odd and beautiful ways. The bass, in short staccatos, reverberated through the hollow of her spine and the harmony of all the treble instruments licked at her skin like a barrage of static shocks. She placed her tiny palms right against the fabric net of the speakers and felt the hums converge together, a dozen lines of sound melting into soup. She loved to feel music. She pressed her back up to the speakers sometimes, let the music under the chamber of her chest and watched as her father danced himself to the beat, swaying his hips and tapping his feet. He was a tall and thin man, short cropped brown hair, and limbs that were long and angular so that when he danced, there was always a sacred geometry mapped by his body.

* * *

When Lily was six, she learned that Miss Rachel was also a special educator at the elementary school and was to be her kindergarten teacher. Every child in Miss Rachel's class was deaf. Two months into the school year, Miss Rachel signed to the class, I have a very special surprise for all of you. The next week, Lily's class took a field trip to the zoo. At each pen she tried her hardest to lean over the railing in order to get as close as possible to each majestic creature. They passed birds of every color and size. There was a whole path walled by pens of bizarre hooved creatures to either side: camels whose hairy backs looked like mounds of hay and antelope crowned with spiraling horns and some strange beast Lily had never seen before that looked like a cross of ox, deer, and goat. The class walked along a high bridge suspended over a vast field of green where in the distance Lily could see the heads of giraffes nested on the canopies of their tree trunk necks. All the hooved animals smelled like the stuff the dog left behind in the lawn and the children began to sign to one another, You smell like a camel! They did this with each new animal and burst into fits of giggles. And, after an hour of walking and stopping and gawking, the class arrived at the primate pen where a family of gorillas was grooming each other quietly.

Lily leaned over the railing. The gorilla pen was rather large and contained in a black wire fence. Between the fence and the overlook railing, her body was now slung over a moat of running water that created a barrier between the two. She squinted in disbelief across the distance, trying to affirm what she thought she saw. Some of the gorillas were making signs with their hands. Now the other children leaned forward. They recognized it too. A dozen tiny heads turned to face a zookeeper dressed in a sand-colored uniform and a pith helmet. As he spoke, he signed. His hands told of the puzzle pieces of life called DNA and how the difference between human and ape was like taking a tiny fraction off only one puzzle piece. Lily marveled.

The zookeeper continued. He signed: A long time ago, scientists taught a couple of gorillas sign language. Remarkably, they learned it. It isn't perfect, but you can make it out. If you have little brothers or sisters, it is a lot like signing to a three year old. They even teach it to their babies now. We try harder every year to increase their understanding. Just imagine what it would be like if humans could actually have conversations with the rest of the world. What would the animals tell us, do you think? That's what the scientists do here: teach enough so that one day the gorillas might tell us how we're doing with this whole ruling the world business.

Draping her body over the railing, her mouth hung open. When she looked back for her mother—who was chaperoning the trip—she could see her engaged in conversation with Miss Rachel.

Miss Rachel said, I always love coming here. It's breathtaking. I can't imagine what it's like for the children, to see another species communicating in their native language.

Lily looked back to the apes. Yes, they *were* signing to each other! The big beast—the mother—was signing to her children, Come. Groom.

Lily leapt excitedly, wildly waving her hands. Hello! Hello!

One young gorilla, no bigger than she was, crawled up to the edge of the gorilla pen and gazed up at her from where the moat began. The gorilla responded, Hello human. Then it bared its teeth and fangs which shocked Lily before she calmed and realized it was smiling at her.

She signed, How are you?

Lily grinned so hard her face hurt. The young gorilla looked like a large infant. Its head was mostly bald; the black hair on its crown was a thin wiry patch of translucent tangles like the dust clouds Lily found underneath the couch. Its eyes were big, round, and surprisingly human-like. She had expected the glassy eyes of her dog, the dumb expression that revealed nothing but the simplest desires: food, play, joy. Even her mother had given the same vacant look before, as if someone had gone and scrubbed out the inside of her head. This most often happened at the doctor's when the white coats were speaking to her mother for a long time in lip patterns Lily couldn't recognize. Sometimes, she'd giggle and try to wake her mother up by tugging at a sleeve or a wisp of her hair or necklace. Then through some sudden sorcery, her mother's eyes would reignite.

The gorilla signed back, Happy. Sign human big. No small.

Lily thought for a second, piecing together the fragmented ideas in her head. She was used to having to reorganize ideas. Before Miss Rachel taught her to sign, she often tried to communicate by combining and recombining lip patterns in different orders to see if her parents could understand better or even recognize her attempts at communication. Though her parents never even looked at her lips, Lily became remarkably good at puzzles. She decided that the gorilla was telling her it was happy to be signing with a child. The thought of the young gorilla's loneliness saddened her until her classmates rushed the railing and a chorus of small hands gestured excitedly to the beasts.

The jaws of each gorilla split into smiles and open laughter. They raised their hands.

* * *

Every day, Lily's father came home from work, sat on the couch and watched TV. Lily often scooted up to her father, climbed onto the brown leather couch and nested herself beside him. He always took a glance at her, curled his lips into a smile and then returned his attention to the television. If she slid herself too close to him, she noticed how he'd begin to lean his body away from her. Lily learned to sit precisely the length of her leg away from her father so that he'd be comfortable. She used to try to sign to him while he watched, hoping to catch his attention, but his gaze only fell to her momentarily. She felt a terrible shame in the way he would avoid looking at her, purposefully and unnaturally fixing his eyes straight ahead when he walked by.

Still, every weekend her father took her to the park. In the distance, two basketball courts took up half the park which Lily and her father always avoided. The young boys all gathered there in contest like gladiators. The other half of the park—their half—was an open field of grass, all green save for patches of sandy dirt freckling the ground. There was a playground in the corner of the field that called to Lily. She raced toward it every weekend, leaving her father on a bench. Her eyes absorbed its architecture. There were swing sets and seesaws and her favorite piece of equipment was a bright red jungle gym sprouting from the earth in a twisted knot of metal. Lily bounced on ground that looked like hard asphalt yet yielded beneath her feet in a strange rubbery way.

Sometimes her father took her into the grass and they threw a baseball between themselves. Most weekends, he sat on the bench and read business magazines when Lily made her dash toward the playground. She always climbed the jungle gym. Climbed and climbed. And when at last she reached the summit of the red tower, she sat across two bars, tiny legs dangling, and watched over the entire park. The bodies below were small and Lily felt a tremendous calm looking down over the park.

At first, Lily tried to play with other children in the park. They were welcoming enough, inviting her in when she noticed their lips moving at her. Eventually though, they stopped. She could see from her high tower perch their lips whispering comments about the weird girl who never spoke. They whispered and then they watched her and then they whispered some more. When they noticed her eyes from above, they turned their backs. Sometimes Lily avoided looking at their mouths. Sometimes she couldn't help herself.

One day, her father ran into a friend of his. The strange man stole glances at Lily as he chatted with her father. She watched her father's lips. He asked the man how he was doing, how the job was going, how the wife and kids were. The man asked all the same questions in return and her father gave his answers in single words: fine; great; good. As the strange man said his goodbyes, he tousled Lily's hair, bending down to her level. With his fat purple chapped lips, he said, Adorable little girl you have here. Lily suddenly clung to her father's leg and turned her head up. She read her father's lips as he said, Oh yes. This is my daughter. She'll be turning seven soon.

* * *

According to Miss Rachel, her father had asked why Lily sat by the speakers or played with his guitars. Miss Rachel explained how Lily loved the feel of the music and becoming part of the sound. After that day, Miss Rachel started staying later. She sat down with Lily's father in the living room, speaking and signing and waiting for him to respond in sign.

It took a year for her father to become the least bit proficient. It was amusing to watch, to see his eyes glow hot with frustration when he failed. Lily was beginning to understand how fundamentally different their worlds were. As far as it mattered to her, sound was still magic, still a supernatural clairvoyant sense. She saw how dependent her father was on sound, how he needed it to organize his world.

Their first conversations were simple. At dinner, he asked how Lily's food was. She replied, but he took the interim to begin eating. Lily had noticed this early with the hearing children at school: when they talked over food, they could take turns. One person spoke and the other ate. It seemed natural and effortless. Lily and her mother had sunk into a different rhythm. When they signed over dinner, it required both to take a break from eating to have a short exchange. Now Lily felt a sting of envy and hurt over her father's inconsideration. She turned to her mother regretfully.

Her mother smiled warmly and pulled back the brunette hair that fell over her face. Lily smiled back. Her mother signed, How was your school day?

Good, replied Lily. The new teacher is having trouble teaching us to read though. I'm glad Miss Rachel still comes here.

Miss Rachel had told her that if she learned to read and write, other people would be able to understand her too. So she applied herself with diligence, studying the careful shapes of letters and how they interacted with one another to create ideas. She quickly realized that this undertaking would be her most difficult. As soon as she felt she had a grasp on a word, casting the text's font into the folds of her mind, Lily would look away from the page and all the letters would dissolve into hills of black sand.

Her mother signed back, It must be hard. Words are in different orders than what you're used to.

And Lily responded with mild offense: They come in the same way that people speak. I read lips all the time. I'm used to that, but not these shapes.

Her mother just didn't get it. Miss Rachel had informed Lily that hearing children sounded words out when they learned to read. It was an alien idea. Lily understood that reading and writing were conventions made for the hearing. Written language was predicated on sound, but she was learning English as a set of pictograms, memorizing whole shapes to represent words and never learning how those words were built. She understood the lip patterns of letters and shapes, but little more. Years later, Lily would learn that children in China learned to read and write *hanzi* in much the same way—rout memorization of symbols—and it was not until then that she would feel less alone.

When Lily and her mother had conversations in the past, her father often sat silently. She could always see the perturbed glint in his eyes, the hidden snarl behind the flat line of his lips, the whole electric aura that radiated from his skin to hers in nasty bitter heat. It elated her when he started to learn sign. At last! Perhaps they would not be so alien to one another anymore.

She felt an ache of longing for her father. It seemed they were always so far apart, both mute in wholly different ways. She was used to the silence of her father, the detached manner of his parenting. She wasn't terribly upset; she noticed too how her father didn't speak much to her mother either, how they often passed each other by with sheepish smiles in the kitchen or in the hall, how her mother read in the bedroom upstairs and he watched TV downstairs. So Lily waited as he forked a bite into his mouth and signed again when he looked up. Immediately he stiffened and an embarrassed pink flushed his cheeks as he realized his folly. He set his fork down in a jerky hesitant movement. In reply, he signed, Sorry. Lily smiled, reassured that his slight was unintentional.

Her mother's lips moved to say, Thank you for trying, dear.

Her father replied, I feel like an idiot.

Learning a whole new language is tough, said Lily's mother. It'll come. It was hard for me too. It still is.

Lily turned back to her food and ate. She let her parents recede from her world; she let them saunter casually back to their own without the intrusion of her gaze.

* * *

Her father took her to the zoo one day after weeks of begging and pleading. She wanted him to share this experience with her, to communicate freely across the barrier of species. She took his hand and led him to the gorilla pen. The young gorilla she had first signed with—named Hermes by the zookeepers—was engaged in a conversation with an older female gorilla. She signed, No game.

Hermes replied, Give food. The female repeated herself emphatically. It looked like Hermes was explaining himself: Game gorillas, food give.

Lily looked up at her father. She wondered if he even recognized the signs. When he squinted and leaned himself forward, she smiled. He signed to her, It's just gibberish.

She shook her head. No, they just don't know the right order. Lily began waving toward Hermes until she had his attention. She signed, Do you remember me? This is my father.

Hermes smiled and replied, Hello human-small. Hello human-big.

She nudged her father. She signed, Have a conversation. Ask him how he is.

Her father was stoic. He stared at Hermes who started signing something about crushed apples. Then he looked back down at Lily and signed, They can't actually communicate. They're just animals, Lily. They're trained with a few words and that's it.

She frowned. The gorillas *could* communicate. She looked over the pen and saw four separate conversations. But then Lily saw the railing, the chasm that had been dug out to create a moat of water and an impassable barrier between the humans and the gorillas. She felt herself floating in the moat, the great gulf built on a fraction of a puzzle piece. When she looked up at her father, she imagined a railing under his nose. He looked down at her and smiled and she felt dirty and feral under his gaze.

* * *

When Lily rushed down the stairs in the morning, turned the corner to cross through the living room into the kitchen, she saw her father on the couch, his body made a fat sausage beneath a blue blanket. She touched his face and he awoke with a start. He smiled. A yellow crust bridged over his eye, connected together his lashes until Lily plucked it away. Her father sat up, folded his arms around her, the blanket cocooning the pair together. Then he stood and Lily watched as his body rounded back the corner to the stairs from which she came.

At the breakfast table, Lily's mother did not sign a greeting to her. There was just a pleasant smile, although it appeared drawn on her face because her eyes were not reacting to her lips. Lily normally felt her mother was beautiful, the way her eyes and hair were both richly chocolate. Today there was purple rubbed in beneath her eyes. She looked haggard. Her gaze never touched Lily again that morning—always, they were either on plates or silverware or food or the clock. When her father returned, dressed and groomed, Lily saw that neither set of lips moved. She saw the quick darting glances her parents stole of each other, the momentary diagonal line their mouths formed that telegraphed some sense of great frustration. Their bodies radiated a heat of quiet animosity which found form in Lily's belly as a raw ache.

Lily discovered a new fact about sound at this breakfast table: silence was a punishment. She remembered the vibrations that channeled through the floorboards last night—she was learning to identify them by feel, force, duration. There were quick strong, rapid booms—a series of stomps like her father marching across the room. She placed her small hand upon the wall and felt mild buzzing akin to when she would hold a tin can to Miss Rachel's mouth and have her sing into it. She went to her door, cracked it open, peeked through the hallway to see her parents' bedroom open, the light on, her mother's face flushed pink, wet with tears, and she was shouting. Her lips read, If you don't love me anymore, why are you even here?

Now her father stepped into Lily's view. He stared down her mother; it was the most menacing glare Lily had ever seen him wear. He spoke slowly, Why do you think? Then he turned toward the hallway. Her father threw the door shut as he left the room. The sound pulsed through the air with violence. It shook her bones.

* * *

Miss Rachel seemed to age in bursts. Each week the color rubbed beneath her eyes became more and more bruised. Hidden behind the frames of her eyeglasses was the attack of crow's feet, visible only when Miss Rachel peeled the frames from her face to rub her eyes, leaving them raw and reddened. Lily felt her father's outbursts of yelling, his pacing stomps, in chaotic vibrations through the floorboards. She could see how much Miss Rachel tried to help and her father's failure to comprehend. One day, Lily peered into the living room to see her father openly sobbing. Miss Rachel hovered over him, smoothing her hand into his back. His lips said, I love her. I really do. This is just so hard. They always say, Stay together for the kids, right? That's what we're supposed to do, right?

That night, Miss Rachel stayed later than she ever had and Lily felt no stomping or yelling. In the morning before she left for school, she hugged her father's waist. He knelt and met her eyes and his weeping came on suddenly, his eyes and his lips all pulled down and when he hugged Lily to his body, she felt his breathing as a series of jolting pops.

* * *

Her father went through waves. Some nights, he was social with her. He made honest attempts at communication. They'd play together. He'd turn up jazz records and she'd sit down by the speaker. As she felt the music run up through her spine, they chattered through sign over simple nonsense.

Her father signed, The dog bit me today.

Grinning, Lily asked, Really?

No, I just learned *bite*, he responded. She giggled, felt the hum of it in her throat, and saw her father smile.

And then, inexplicably and for stretches, her father grew distant, pretending Lily wasn't there or—worse—simply not noticing. Lily did not know if she was the problem or if her mother was. Any interaction, like their weekend park trip, seemed forced and his affection feigned. She felt little more than an animal to her father, some half-aware creature he could placate by throwing a ball around. Lily saw it wearing on him: having to introduce her to his friends with a disclaimer. This is my *deaf* daughter, he told a woman once in the park. The woman blinked in shock, stiffened unnaturally, and then gave a sweeping and overdone show of sympathy. Lily hated the woman for it. When she looked back to her father, she saw how he had stitched a smile over his face. His words were superficially cheerful; his lips revealed a private calamity.

* * *

And then one day, he was gone. His drawers had been emptied. His toothbrush vanished. He left behind a scribble on a scrap of paper left on the kitchen table. For all of Lily's progress in reading, she could only make sense of trivial words. *I'm. Go. My. You. The.* Miss Rachel, when she heard the news, showered

Lily with sympathetic attention. Her mother lavished her with toys and treats—Oreos and peanut butter cups and ice cream sandwiches.

It didn't stop the confusion.

Lily tried figure out this new order, but the pieces didn't fit. They jarred inside her like bad cheese. She clung to memories of her father, retreating to the empty basement at night, sliding chairs across the floor so she could climb atop them and finger the padded hooks of the now barren wall mounts. Shadow outlines of guitars stained the walls. Each day, she returned home to find more and more relics of her phantom father receding from their home. The albums all vanished in a day, leaving square slots naked. It was unsettling to be able to see the wall so easily through the shelf. Her mother later placed banal ornaments in their place: snow globes, small picture frames, a tiny porcelain statue of a gorilla they had purchased on the zoo trip. It felt to Lily like blowing air into the spaces left by her father.

Miss Rachel continued to visit at least two evenings a week. Lily felt it was as much for herself as her mother. When Lily asked of her father, Miss Rachel only replied that he went away. Her mother wouldn't reply at all.

* * *

She remembered her father's distant days, his defeated posture in the park, his total ignorance of his own daughter. She wondered secretly how terrible a burden she was. One day at school, in the cafeteria where the children ate lunch, Lily had spotted a table of children all propped up with their knees on their seats, leaning their bodies hungrily over the table and passing a pair of dice between them. One child shook his fist into the air and dropped the dice. All the children then roared up, cocking their heads back with jaws agape in laughter. Lily approached and peered between the heads and shoulders of children. On the table was a board with an arrangement of colored squares.

A number of the squares had tiny colored plastic pieces resting atop them and, at the board's center, two thick decks of cards stood side-by-side like skyscrapers over the pieces.

Lily gently nestled her way between bodies, eager to join in their game. The boy across the table met her gaze. He asked, Who's the girl?

A brunette girl beside him answered, I think she's one of the deaf kids from the Special Hall. I've seen her around.

Lily thought that the kids kept chattering on about her, but she couldn't move her eyes fast enough to catch anyone's lips. She followed their eyes though, moving from one child to another. There was definitely a conversation. Finally, she saw the first boy say: Ignore her. She can watch all she wants. We don't have to let her play. With that, another child launched the dice onto the board.

Lily turned away, withdrawing back to her table with her classmates where she felt some semblance of *normal*. She should have been used to it, the way the children in the park had come to exclude her. Today, she felt weak. Today, the weight of her isolation was crushing. Today, the world felt especially cruel, especially unfair, especially volatile.

Distraught, bewildered, Lily rushed home at the day's end, sped up the stairs and into her room, waiting until the sun set and cast her room, the hall, the house in darker shades of blue. Waiting until she saw light bleed up the stairwell to tell her that her mother had finally returned home. And then Lily descended in a fury, tears streaming and hands frantic. A blur of fingers and knuckles and fists. Her mother hugged her and Lily drank in the scent of strawberry-melon shampoo, nestled her face into her mother's shoulder and hair.

Later, after she had calmed, Lily signed, It will always be this way, won't it? I'm a freak. And then she collapsed into a puddle on the carpet.

Her mother stroked Lily's hair and mouthed in front of her eyes, You are incredibly special. Now she pulled away, held Lily by the shoulders and her face grew grave so that Lily knew to pay attention. She said, I want you to understand, Lily, that none of this is your fault.

But Lily was not so sure. For all of her ability to pick up a conversation from across the room, to read the buried twists and twitches of a person's lips, there were things she could never hear or understand: how she cleaved the love between her mother and father in two; what dug the vast lacuna between her father and herself; how being human felt.

* * *

Weeks later, Miss Rachel took Lily back to the zoo. She wanted to see the gorillas again. Lily stood at the railing and gazed down over the beasts, watching their conversations. The gorillas signed in shards of words and ideas and metaphors that made her laugh breathlessly to herself. The younger apes signed upward to the humans on the overlook, trying desperately to be understood. Lily did not respond. Miss Rachel signed, You aren't going to sign to the gorillas?

This caused the young apes to start signing more frantically. Lily stepped back from the railing so she couldn't be seen. She smiled and shook her head. No, she signed.

She didn't explain. She didn't know the words to tell Miss Rachel why she had wanted to come here. Lily returned to watching the fragmented conversations of the animals. She wanted to experience the gulf between them. She imagined a future life: Lily, the adult; Lily, the scientist; Lily, the bridge between humanity and the rest of the world. Maybe someday, between her mother and father too. She imagined ripping away all the invisible railings in the world. She saw herself filling up that moat with dirt, mud, soil, and all the richness of the earth.

Empty Apartments

Sarah Bridgins

Sophie's affair with her boss begins slowly, to the point where after a few months she is simultaneously convinced the attraction she feels is mutual and certain that it's all in her head.

Sophie is not the type of person who has an affair. At twenty-one she is just growing out of her high school shyness. She didn't drink in college, and while her friends were busy going out and meeting guys she spent most nights writing poetry about visiting art museums alone and organizing her bookshelf according to which writers she thought would want to hang out with each other. In some ways, the fact that her boss has a wife and kid makes the whole thing easier. She can spend hours obsessing over something he's said or a gesture he's made, but in reality there is no ambiguity behind anything he does. He has a family. All she has is time.

After a while, it becomes hard to dismiss the afternoons they spend lingering at each other's desks as professional friendliness.

At forty, Ben seems closer to her age than he does to the other people they work with. He listens to the Pixies, occasionally comes in hung over, and still has no idea what he wants to do with his life. Because his job in publishing does not pay enough to support a family of three in Manhattan he also does some real estate work on the side. He is not very good at this and talks about quitting both jobs almost every day. Before he came to New York he spent five years teaching American literature in Japan. While there, he learned to speak Japanese and traveled to ten different countries. He has stories about being taught how to juggle by a beautiful bald woman on a beach in Israel and of fighting off stag beetles the size of his palm in a tent in Thailand. He often jokes with Sophie about running off together to somewhere exotic and living in a hut in the countryside. Sophie knows he is kidding, but that doesn't keep her from daydreaming about the morning he will come in with his bags packed and announce they are leaving.

* * *

Ben kisses Sophie after a coworker's birthday party. The whole department goes out for drinks after work and by 8:00 they are all drunk. Sophie sits next to Ben, pressing her knee against his and when he walks her to the subway at the end of the night they start making out like teenagers.

The next day at the office Sophie is convinced that everyone knows what happened. This is both terrifying and thrilling. For a moment she wishes she had someone there to talk to about it.

Sophie has been at her job for three months. She is an assistant at a publishing house in Tribeca that specializes in paranormal romance novels. Ben is the editor she works with. While most of her friends were smart enough to leave the city after graduation, she found a place off of Craigslist and moved to the East Village. The apartment is the size of a refrigerator box, lets in no natural light, and costs her half a month's salary in rent. Because it is impossible to be there for more than ten minutes at a stretch without becoming clinically depressed, she and her roommate have developed a routine that involves getting drunk on her bedroom floor and complaining about the lack of mentally stable men in New York. Although it probably isn't as healthy as say, taking up knitting or revising her five-year plan to include something more ambitious than not getting any regrettable tattoos, Sophie's life has felt so pathetic that having an ill-fated crush on her married boss seemed like a welcome distraction.

So far the closest Sophie has come to making friends is a thirty-year-old assistant named Tamara who makes jewelry at her desk and occasionally asks Sophie to eat lunch with her in an empty conference room. The rest of the office is made up of middle-aged mothers who commute in from New Jersey. When Sophie and Ben left together the night before, she noticed Bunny, the head of the department, glaring at her. Bunny is forty-five years old and has the disingenuous friendliness of someone under the impression that the campaign for prom queen continues after high school. She seems suspicious of Sophie because Sophie is half her age and always comes to work overdressed.

In the afternoon, Ben calls Sophie into his office. She can't tell if he is going to apologize or proposition her. Finally he whispers:

"I'm not really sure how to bring this up, but I had a nice time last night. I wanted to see how you felt about it. Are you okay?"

"I feel great."

"I know what I've been thinking, I just want to make sure that this is all fair to you. What do you want?"

"I want you."

As soon as she says this she knows it is mistake. Ben's eyes drop to his desk and he starts nervously playing with a paper clip.

"You know you can't have that right? I mean, with everything else going on. I want this to work, but I don't want to hurt you."

"You won't. I promise."

Ben looks at her.

"I have keys to empty apartments around the city that we could use to meet up in. God, I'm probably turning red as a tomato right now. It would just be until I figured something else out. I just have some time management issues to work on."

Sophie's head feels fuzzy. She wonders if anyone has ever used the phrase "time management" before when discussing adultery. In her fantasies, this conversation was much hotter. Ben would tell her he couldn't stop thinking about her, and they would run off to her apartment and have sex in her loft bed while somehow avoiding hitting their heads on the ceiling. This feels more like a business transaction that has no chance of working out in her favor.

"Okay," she says, "that sounds good."

* * *

The apartment they go to is on Christopher Street. She can hear him talking to someone at his real estate office in the morning, and at noon he slips over to her cubicle and gives her a folded piece of paper.

"I'm leaving to pick up the keys." he whispers, his face close enough to lick. "Meet me here in fifteen minutes."

She nods, feeling like a cross between a secret agent and a hooker.

When she gets to the building he is standing outside twirling a set of keys on his index finger. Neither of them says anything as they go in, but in the lobby he puts his hand on her waist.

They walk into the apartment and are suddenly shy. Now that they are there it is unclear exactly what they are about to do. Will they have sex? Where? The apartment is large and unfurnished with a fireplace and a garden out the back door. Because it is basement-level she can see people's feet walking by outside the windows. The room is empty except for a hammer left by a maintenance man that lies on the floor looking somehow accusatory.

Ben puts his hand on her shoulder and she turns to face him. He takes off her green coat and, in what feels like an oddly formal gesture, drapes it across the kitchen counter. This breaks the tension. Ben kisses her and soon they are pulling at each other's clothes, frantically reaching for zippers, buttons, and belts like parachuters grasping for ripcords.

"Lie down," he says.

Sophie lies down on the floor. Logistics no longer seem important, and she barely notices the cold of the hardwood on her back.

He starts licking her, slowly at first, then speeding up. Although it feels good, Sophie knows the chances of the apartment being bombed in a nuclear attack are far greater than those of her having an orgasm. She is always nervous being with someone new and the stark setting doesn't help. She wiggles around and makes moaning noises for a while and when it seems like it's been long enough that his feelings won't get hurt, she sits up. Ben sits up too and leans his back against the wall. He starts to say something, but she kisses him on his neck, then his stomach, before working her way down and putting her mouth on him.

When they are done, Ben lies down.

"Come here," he says, looking up at her and holding out his arm for her to join him.

Sophie lies down next to him. He curls the outstretched arm around her and she puts her head on his chest. He strokes her back then kisses the top of her head.

It is the first chance she has had to get a full look at Ben's naked body. His arms and legs are thin and muscular, but he has a small potbelly that makes her feel oddly protective of him.

"You are amazing," he says. "I feel like I'm on drugs right now. I don't think I've felt this way since college."

He kisses her again, then rolls onto his side so that she is looking at him.

"How are you? Are you okay?"

Sophie kisses his chest. "Of course I'm okay. Why wouldn't I be?"

The more he asks if she is okay, the less okay she feels, but the more she wants him to think that she is.

"I don't know. I just want to make sure this isn't too much for you. Also, you didn't finish."

"I'm fine, I promise. I just don't that often."

This is and is not a lie. Sophie has no problem getting off by herself, but she has never been able to with another person. In college she only slept with two guys, neither of whom she dated for more than a month. The first was a biochemistry major who seemed to regard her body as a math problem he couldn't figure out, and the second was a self-absorbed actor who had little patience for any orifice incapable of complimenting him.

"Oh," Ben says looking relieved. "Well we can fix that. We'll just have to practice a lot."

"That sounds good to me." The suggestion of more time together gives her a small rush.

"Hey, you want to know something?" he asks.

"Absolutely."

"I used to have my ears pierced. Both of them. In college. I also had long hair that I wore in a ponytail and once I put a blue streak in it. It used to be blond then if you can believe it." He smiles at her as though he has just made some kind of intimate post-coital confession, and Sophie is struck with the sense that the man he wants her to see is the same one who is fifteen years younger and still has the time to run marathons, learn Japanese, and read two books a week. She decides she is okay with this as even the ghost of who he used to be is better than the nothing she has now.

"I like the way it looks now." She runs her fingers through his graying hair. "I think it's sexy."

He laughs and pulls her closer, and she discovers that she is, in fact, feeling okay. He doesn't seem too concerned about all of this, so why should she be? She expected the whole thing to feel more serious, more illicit, but lying next to him does not feel so different from the few other men she has been with. It feels nice. She decides that maybe she was wrong, that maybe she is tougher than she thought she was and that maybe she can do this. Then Ben stirs and her heart does an uncomfortable flutter.

"It's getting late. We should head back. I can leave first so we don't walk in together."

He stands up and she is amazed at how quickly she can go from okay to awful. "Okay," she says, not moving. "When do you think I'll see you again? I mean, I see you every day, but— you know what I mean."

"I know, I've thought about that and I still have some more things I have to figure out, but I will. Don't worry." He stares at her then shakes his head. "You are unbelievably beautiful."

This is the first time anyone has ever told her this and the effect is disorienting. While part of her is panicking that this will all be a disaster, part of her immediately, stupidly, trusts him.

"Now come on," he says gently, reaching out his hand, "get up."

* * *

When Sophie gets home that night her roommate Esme is sitting next to their kitchen window smoking. Esme is a Gender Studies major at NYU. The first week Sophie moved in they stayed up all night discussing their high school eating disorders and giddily reading aloud to each other from a thirty-year-old collection of Andy Rooney essays that Esme had found in the trash on her way home. Then one night Sophie went to bed early and Esme woke her up at 2 a.m. to ask her what flavor cupcake she would be if given the choice. Sophie realized she needed to establish some boundaries.

Tonight, however, Sophie is relieved to have someone to talk to. She sits down on the windowsill and tells Esme about her afternoon, leaving out as many details as possible. After she is finished she takes one of Esme's cigarettes and lights it.

"Am I a bad person?"

"No, you're just a stupid person. And a self-destructive one. Also, you don't smoke. You're going to hurt yourself if you keep waving it around like that."

"I'm stressed out."

"I'm going to be stressed out too if you burn the apartment down. What are you hoping to get out of this anyway? Do you want him to leave his wife for you?"

"God no, that would be a disaster. He has a kid."

"Well then what's the point? You know you could do better right? You could throw a rock out this window and find someone who's less of an asshole than he is. And we're in the East Village."

"I don't want better. I want Ben." Sophie takes a drag of her cigarette, but only half inhales.

"Wow that's sad. In that case I only have one piece of advice: don't give him a blow job."

"Why not?"

"I don't know, but every time I give a guy a blow job they seem to disappear. You have to keep him wanting more. Have you ever seen a picture of his wife? Or his kid? What's his wife's name?"

"Her name is Ally. He used to have a picture of both of them as his computer background, but he changed it. She's pretty. They started dating in high school, but they've only been married five years."

"Okay, maybe you are a bad person. And I'm taking these away from you."

Esme takes her cigarettes off the windowsill and goes into her room.

"Goodnight!" she shouts. "I have some Xanax in the bathroom if you need one!"

It takes Sophie hours to fall asleep. She lies in bed listening to the cockroaches skitter around in the kitchen and to the drunk college kids stumbling along E. 7th Street She thinks about what Esme said, how she could do better, and wonders why it is impossible for her to believe it. Drifting off to sleep a couple hours before dawn, the reasoning she goes with is this: Does a person on a desert island turn away a rescue boat just because they know it might eventually sink?

* * *

Something Sophie discovers: your day goes by much faster when you are having an affair with your boss. Mornings are spent sitting in her cubicle outside Ben's office wondering when he will come out, say hi to her, and notice the adorable, but work-inappropriate dress she's wearing. Often this takes a while, as they have both agreed to talk less when they're at work. For the past few weeks, whenever Bunny notices that Sophie is in Ben's office she makes it a point to come in and ask about his son. Whenever Bunny does this, Sophie is forced back to her desk and is too nervous to go back to Ben's office for the rest of the morning. This is painful and it suddenly seems very urgent that he know all about the vegetarian burrito that exploded in her microwave and how her cat has started to come when she calls it *as if it thinks it's a dog.*

Ben can only get away once or twice a week. On the weeks when he is unable to get the keys to an apartment, they are forced to meet in a storage room where copies of old books are kept. The first few times they do this Sophie is terrified. However, Ben assures her that he has the only key to the room and soon sneaking in there feels as normal as anything else they do.

The room is small and lined with metal shelving that holds dusty copies of books with titles like *Boyz That Bite* and *Wolf in Hunk's Clothing*. There is a copy machine down the same hallway and sometimes Sophie can hear its steady *beep beep* when Ben is going down on her. This used to distract her, but she learns to focus on the noise in a way that helps her get off with him for the first time.

They are both shocked when this happens. She has been getting closer for weeks, but assumed that actually finishing would be impossible given how nerve-wracking their meetings are.

Ben takes his head out from under her dress. Sophie is sitting on a swivel chair that someone stored in the corner of the room, and Ben is kneeling in front of her. He is grinning.

"That was amazing," he says. "Goddamn, you were great."

"Yeah? I hope I didn't take too long."

"Are you kidding? You're perfect." Ben puts his head back under her dress and kisses her.

Sophie smiles. Part of her feels closer to Ben while another part of her feels like the sole inhabitant of a planet that is thousands of miles away. For the first time she is grateful that they haven't had sex.

She pushes his head out from between her legs.

"We need to figure something out."

"What do you mean?"

"This isn't working. I hate that this happened here. Why can't I see you after work?"

Ben kisses her knee. "I know you do Sophie. I hate it too. I'm working on it, I promise, but I have to be home to take care of Jun."

As soon as Ben mentions his son, Sophie knows she's lost. What kind of an asshole would argue with that?

Ben takes her hand. "I feel the same way you do. I want to be like the blueberries in your muffin this morning; scattered through every part of your life, not just in one place."

Sophie doesn't know what to think. Is it possible to mean something that makes so little sense? At the same time, the fact that Ben speaks in metaphors is one of the things that attracts her to him. He makes the effort to inject even the smallest bit of poetry into her life. So many people don't even try.

When he leaves for the day Sophie runs into the bathroom, sits in her favorite stall, and spends twenty minutes crying about the mess she's gotten into. There was a time when she also cried about the fact that she'd become one of those women who are so fragile they can't make it through a regular work day without needing to take a break to sob in the bathroom. Then she realized she has always been one of those women, she just hasn't always had a job.

* * *

It gets to the point where Sophie stops being jealous of other people's relationships and starts becoming jealous of their affairs. She reads countless short stories about neurotic young women who have fallen in love with married men, and while she takes comfort in sympathizing with their emotional turmoil she often finds herself focusing on the details of their infidelities rather than the consequences. She can only dream of a world that includes hours spent in seedy hotel rooms and pleading voice mails left in the middle of the night.

Sophie tells him this over wine after work. It is the first time during their three-month affair that she has seen him at night. She reveals her diminished expectations in desperation when, after two hours he says he has to leave.

"Wait, I'm confused, who else do you know that's having an affair?"

"There are people."

"Well of course there are people, but what people? Your friends?"

"No, not my friends. People out there." Sophie says, gesturing crazily with her wine glass. "In books, in movies, in the world. And they're all doing things we're not; going out at night, calling each other, *fucking*."

On this last word she leans over and slaps her hand on his leg, high up on his thigh. She thinks it might embarrass him, this reminder that in three months they haven't even slept together. He has given no reason for this, and Sophie has never pressed the point. Esme told Sophie that sleeping with her must cross some arbitrary moral line, and Sophie has told herself that she does not want to have sex with Ben until they are no longer restricted to empty apartments and supply rooms. At the moment though, Sophie simply wants to make him feel awkward.

Instead of being shaken, Ben just does what he always does when she becomes upset or emotional. He softens his eyes in adoration and says something sentimental that makes no sense.

"That's why I have to go Sophie. Because I care about you and I want *our* story to end well."

He brushes her hair away from her face then kisses her forehead.

"You know you can see someone else if you want to. I just want you to be happy. Sometimes I feel like all I do is upset you."

"I am seeing someone else. A doctor. We went out this week."

Kevin is a medical student Sophie met at a party Esme talked her into going to. He is very cute and when he asked for her number Sophie imagined how great it would be to go on a normal date with someone her age. Instead, he arrived at the bar half an hour late and announced that Sophie would have to pay for everything because he had lost his debit card. When she appeared irritated he rolled his eyes and said, "Come on

Sweetheart. It's only money." She felt like she was going to cry, and went home twenty minutes later.

"How was it? Do you like him?"

"It just made me miss you."

"Aw Sophie. Well, I'm not going to lie. The thought of you out on a date makes me a little jealous."

Sophie wonders if he is saying this to make her feel better. Thinking this makes her feel worse.

"I have an idea," Ben says. "Why don't we set up a time at night when we can think of each other? What about nine o'clock? At nine o'clock I'll stop whatever I'm doing and you'll know that I'm thinking about you, and I'll know that you're doing it too."

This is stupid. It is the kind of thing a fifteen-year-old girl who has just watched *West Side Story* would dream up to ease the loneliness of living two states away from the boyfriend she met at summer camp. Sophie also knows it is the biggest consolation she is going to get so she accepts it.

That night, she sits on her front stoop smoking Esme's cigarettes and watching beautiful young people going in and out of the bars and restaurants on her block. She forgets to check when it is nine.

* * *

For Sophie's birthday Ben takes her to lunch in the Meatpacking District. The restaurant he picks is owned by a very famous chef and serves food that is inspired by Japanese street snacks, but costs five hundred times more. Although Sophie would prefer to see Ben after work she knows that is not likely to happen and does not feel like getting into an argument. When Ben slips her a note that morning with the name of where their reservation is she figures she might as well get excited about it.

The restaurant is huge, with a dining room that is dark and cavernous. As soon as they sit down, Ben slides a package towards her. It is small and square and wrapped in paper covered with Christmas trees. The surprise on her face is genuine. She had not thought he would get her anything.

"I hope you like it. I tried really hard to find something that I thought you would buy."

Sophie unwraps the box. Inside is a sparkly black bracelet that looks like it could have come from any one of the ten thousand stores in the five blocks surrounding their office. She does not care. She puts it on and he looks happy when she tells him that she loves it.

By the time the check comes things start to go downhill.

For the past few weeks Sophie has been getting upset about three quarters of the way through their lunches together. Lately most of what she gets has just been reminding her of what she does not. She does not want two hours. She wants five. Or ten. Or fifty. She wants some kind of impossible arrangement where he does not leave his wife, but she can still somehow wake up with him.

"Why can't we ever go out at night together?"

"We do sometimes."

"The last time was months ago. All you do is lie."

"I tell you things that I think are true at the time. It's not my fault if they don't work out the way I want them to. I would never lie to you."

Sophie stares at her water glass.

"Sophie, why are you doing this? It's your birthday. Can't this just be nice?"

The waiter brings the check. Sophie walks outside without waiting for Ben. The street in front of the restaurant is cobblestone and she is both drunk and wearing high heels. She wobbles along like a person on an unsteady ship, but when Ben runs up and offers to carry her on his back she snaps that no, she is fine.

Ten seconds later she is on the ground. Her broken red heel lies behind her looking like something that's been amputated.

After making sure she is okay, Ben takes off her shoes then lifts her onto his back. He is surprisingly strong and when he picks her up Sophie feels like a child. In desperation she allows herself to do something she never has.

Arms tight around him, face bobbing next to his she asks in a timid unrecognizable voice, "Do you love your wife?"

Ben's gait does not slow. When they reach the other side of the street he sets her down on the sidewalk. In her bare feet she is four inches shorter.

"Well?" she asks.

He looks at her like she is something small and sad, like a kitten missing an eye.

"Yes," he says, "I do love her. Come on Cookie," he adds softly. "We've known each other since we were kids. There's a history there."

Sophie's heart clenches and she feels like she has swallowed an inflated balloon. He has not told her something she did not already know. For a moment, she wonders if her feelings for him are stronger than she'd thought they were. Standing there barefoot in the street though, part of her knows, or at least hopes, that love is both more and less complicated than this.

* * *

Six months in, they begin to lose their sense of discretion. While they still occasionally go to apartments in the neighborhood, Ben's manager has begun asking why he has so many showings, yet never manages to close any deals. As a result, they start going to the storeroom almost every day. First for twenty minutes, then thirty, until eventually they are disappearing for an hour.

Sophie knows that this is stupid, that they are asking to get caught. At this point though, her world has been so completely reduced to their relationship that she often forgets the things that they are doing are going on in real life. Over the past few months, however, even she has noticed the looks she is getting from the other women every time she goes into Ben's office or he stops by her cubicle. One day, when they have been gone an especially long time, Tamara comes over to her desk.

"I need to talk to you, but we can't do it here. Come get coffee with me."

Sophie follows her outside. When they get to the café across the street Tamara stops.

"I overheard something, and I wasn't sure if I should tell you. But I like you, and thought you should probably know."

"What is it?" Sophie can feel her face turn pale.

"You can't disappear any more. When you were gone just now Bunny went into my boss' office and went off about how she knows something is going on with you and Ben. She told Esther that you're always gone at the same time and that she's sure you're sneaking around in the building. It was insane. She had the door closed, but I could hear her yelling."

Sophie is dizzy. Her head feels like it has been stuffed with cotton, and she can feel her hands shaking.

"I know she's wrong," Tamara says slowly, "but you should be careful all the same."

"This is crazy. Sometimes I have to do filing, and Ben is away from his desk all the time. He shows apartments in the middle of the day." Sophie is shocked by her ability to be indignant about being accused of something she is guilty of.

Tamara and Sophie walk back to the office in silence. When she gets to her cubicle Ben can tell that something is wrong.

"We need to talk," Sophie mouths.

Two hours later they are sitting on a bench by the Hudson River. They have made sure to leave the office separately. Sophie tells him what Tamara said.

"It's not like they have any proof. We could be anywhere. I'm always running around doing things," Ben says.

He tells her not to worry, that he will figure things out, but she has long since realized that this is a skill he is not very good at and just thinking about it leaves her exhausted.

* * *

For one month they avoid each other at the office. It is torture. Without him to talk to every day she is forced to face the fact that she has made no other friends at work. Even Tamara has stopped asking her to lunch.

They still manage to meet once a week, and Sophie spends most days stealing glances into his office and having flashbacks of things they've done together, like someone who has been to war.

One morning he comes over to her cubicle like he used to.

"I got a job," he whispers.

She stares at him, confused.

"It's something I applied for months ago, doing in-house copywriting for a construction firm. I never thought I'd get it, but they called me yesterday to tell me I've got the job. The salary is twice as much," he pauses. "I thought about not taking it, but with everything going on here, I feel like I have to."

Sophie sits there, dazed. She has never considered that he might leave, and hearing him say this she is hit with the full weight of just how much she hates her job.

* * *

The last time they go out is to a bar. Ben offers to take Sophie to lunch, but she tells him she isn't hungry. Instead he buys her Jack and ginger ales. Halfway through the third she asks him how he feels about her and if he's sad he's leaving. In response, he draws a picture on the napkin that is sitting in front of him that looks like a pile of sticks.

"Have you ever been camping?" he asks.

She puts her hand on his knee. "Not since third grade. I went with my Brownie troop and came home covered in mosquito bites. I don't think that counts."

He stares at the napkin and gives a small smile.

"The way you build a campfire is by gathering a bunch of sticks and stacking them together like this. Then you fill in the spaces between them with balls of paper and trash. When those burn up the whole thing collapses. That," he says, "is how I feel."

* * *

On Ben's last day they go to the apartment on Christopher Street that they first hooked up in. Sophie has thought about asking him how they will see each other once he leaves, but she knows that any answer he gives will only depress her and she is tired of being lied to. He could barely make time for her when they worked two feet from each other. How is he supposed to manage it from thirty blocks downtown?

Sophie knows this is the last chance they will have to be alone together. Because of this, she has worn her tiniest most uncomfortable pair of underwear, the light blue ones with the pink lace that makes her feel like a sexy five-year-old. These were a very optimistic choice, however, because as soon as he opens the door she starts to cry and she knows that he will not see them.

He takes her hand and leads her toward the middle of the room where he holds her. For a second Sophie feels ridiculous. That does not make this less devastating. She is standing by the counter he sometimes lifts her on to, and she actually becomes nostalgic, as if what she is staring at is the site of their first date or the place where they first met; something that is in any way romantic instead of a slab of Formica where he gave her an orgasm approximately four times a month.

Sophie nuzzles her head into Ben's chest and he pulls her closer. He strokes her hair and whispers, "I'm going to miss you so much. I'm going to find a way to make this work, I promise. I need you. You're the woman I wish I'd met ten years ago. I mean, I know you would have been a kid, but—you know what I mean."

He kisses her forehead and begins to cry too. Sophie has no idea if anything he has just said is what she has been waiting to hear. It doesn't matter. She glances up at the empty room wondering what she will do when he's gone, and her stomach drops, not because things are over, but because they had never really begun.

Beautiful, Terrible Thing

Erika T. Wurth

Mike and Sam had been friends for a while now. At first it had seemed like a strange match. Sam was, more or less, a pretty good kid. Mike on the other hand, was not. He put on a great show however. His beautiful, thick black hair was cut every month by a stylist in Denver that his mother took him to. His clothes were bought from the places in the mall that sharp, masculine but youthful cologne was perpetually emanating from. His grades were perfect.

Honestly, Sam had envied Mike when he first joined track and saw Mike laughing by the side with all of his friends before practice. Mike seemed like the most polished boy he'd ever known. Sam felt awkward and well—sweaty—most of the time. He had friends, even a girlfriend, but considered himself only vaguely popular. He was invited to parties, he could say that. But he was nothing like Mike. Mike had somehow made himself into one of the most well liked kids at Clear Creek, despite the fact that most people knew almost nothing about him. Even his closest friends, if you could call them that. But they knew more than Mike's parents or teachers, or any adults in Mike's life did. What they didn't know was that Mike would do anything. Any drug, any woman—he'd take any risk, and he'd survive, again and again. Sometimes, Mike reminded Sam of Cary, his new girlfriend, in this way.

He loved Cary, and had no idea why Cary had decided to let Sam be her boyfriend, especially considering how their courtship had begun, with Sam barfing in front of her at a party, and then telling her he loved her. But he did. He still trembled when he touched her long, thick orangey brown hair, his hand running all over her copper colored skin like an ocean, a song.

Sam would always sigh deeply whenever they finished having sex and Cary would laugh and light a cigarette and offer him one. At first he said no, thinking back to all of the times he'd promised his mother that he would never smoke, as his biological father had. But pretty quickly, he became curious, and said yes. He was pretty sure that his mother could smell it on him and suspected the truth. He would always tell her that Cary and his other friends would smoke around him and that he never did. At first this had been the truth.

He knew that his mother disliked Cary. She had even gone as far one day as to say that he didn't have to go out with her just because they were both Indian. She had regretted saying this the minute it had left her mouth. Sam had stormed into his room and screamed, "You will *never* understand!" and had slammed his door, and threw on the only powwow tape that he had. He honestly didn't really like it that much. He was more into The Clash.

He had also regretted saying this as soon as it left his mouth. Sam had never known his father, though he enjoyed going to the Ute reservation and hanging out with his family there. He was even learning to speak Ute, and had participated in several ceremonies, which he was very proud of. But he knew that although his mother had loved his biological father deeply, and had been the one to initiate taking Sam to the rez nearly the minute that she understood that his father would never be coming back to do that himself, that they were separated by race was probably one of the most painful things that she dealt with when it came to him.

Both of them had apologized, after Sam had laid on his bed until dinner. But the fact remained that she didn't understand that part of him, and that it would always lie between the two of them, a wide, deep canyon that they both pretended wasn't there.

* * *

"Sam, I really think you should go to this party," Mike said, leaning into his leg and stretching. They were about to run. The sun was bright that day and Sam had to squint to see Mike clearly.

Sam sighed deeply, just like his mother. "I don't know. I really need to study for this test tomorrow." Mike laughed. Sam reached over into the brush that grew not far from the confines of the track and pulled a leaf off of a bush. He stared at it, at the veins growing out from the center of the leaf. He lifted it to his nose and breathed in. Mike plucked the leaf from his fingers and looked at it briefly and with a kind of detached curiosity before he crushed it and tossed the remnants back into the side of the mountain.

"Oh, come on. You know the material. It can't be that hard," Mike smiled at him and Sam looked into eyes that were even darker and more slanted than his own. Mike was so entirely beautiful, he almost wasn't there.

"Well… okay," Sam said. He knew that Cary would go, and though he never had any reason not to trust her, he had to admit that he wanted to be out with her, whenever any other men were involved.

"That's the Sam I know and love," Mike said, patting Sam on the back. It was Sam's turn to laugh, as he knew that neither of those things were true at all.

They hit the track, and Sam could see that Mike was having trouble, again. It bothered Mike deeply, as he was the star. He was used to winning. But lately, there was pain, Sam could tell.

He knew what it was. Sam was an average runner, but he'd been doing it for so long that he had begun to recognize the signs of someone whose bones had begun to rebel. The strangest part about it was that often it was the ones who'd been the best runners who ended up being unable to run long term. Sam, however, was doing better and better. He never pushed himself and always took it slow. The coach, and the other runners, including Mike, had begun to notice his gradual improvement.

He looked over at Mike after his run, and smiled uneasily, not wanting Mike to feel bad and not knowing the borders, the limits of Mike's masculinity. But Mike smiled back, and pulled his long brown fingers through his hair. "I need a cigarette," he said irreverently, sitting down on one of the shitty wooden benches on the side of the track. The brown paint was peeling off of the bench, and that bench in particular looked like it was always on the verge of collapsing. Sam laughed. "Me too," he said, though ever since he'd started, he wanted to stop.

* * *

"Mom. Mom! Look… it's a Thursday. And I'm a senior …" he was on the phone with his mother, and it wasn't going well. He was on the pay phone in the hallway, the one across from the gym. He could hear the squeak of tennis shoes on rubber coming from the double doors. It was women's basketball practice and those girls were vicious.

"Mom, I can spend the night at Cary's," he said, turning around and leaning on the phone. "Yes, Mom, I'm being safe," he said, covering the phone and whispering.

"I said I'm being safe… safe!" He said, yelling, and attracting the attention of two girls walking by. They looked at each other and giggled.

"Mom, look, I'm not gonna get anyone in trouble, okay. You know me. I'm … I … always do the right thing. Just because I have some new friends doesn't mean they're going to change who I am." He listened to her silence and waited for her to speak. He ran his hands through his dark brown hair and then shook his head.

"I promise. Mom, please. You can't keep me a child forever. Next year I'm going to college, and you can't be by my side making my decisions for me then, can you?" She began to laugh and he breathed a sigh of relief. They talked for a few more minutes before he put the phone on the hook. He leaned against the phone for a minute, and thought about Cary. He was supposed to meet her at Beau Jo's in half an hour.

As he made his way out of the school, he saw Mike talking to a girl. Or more like, she was talking to him and he was nodding and looking off into the distance. This, Sam thought, would be the moment a girl would take off to tell her friends what a jerk Mike was for not really paying attention to her. But they never did. They always kept talking to Mike, no matter how he acted, what he said.

"Hey Mike," he said, coming up to them both. She was a short girl, rather plain. Beside her, Mike's beauty was even larger. But Mike seemed to like these kinds of girls the most. And it wasn't as if he necessarily went for the smart ones either. He generally seemed to draw the girls who perpetually held their arms across their chests, the girls who flinched involuntarily every time you made a sharp movement with your hand.

"Hey," Mike said, looking relieved to see him. The girl, Sara, did not.

"Cigarette?" Mike asked and Sam nodded. It was clear that the girl was not invited but she started to walk with them anyway. Mike stopped and turned to her.

"Well. Good talking with you."

She blinked a few times, and then said, "Oh, okay, later." And she walked away, turning her head around several times, clearly hoping Mike would turn back. He did not.

"So, are you, uh, seeing that girl?" Sam asked awkwardly, pushing the first set of double doors open, and holding them open for Mike. Mike laughed.

"No," he said, pushing through the second set, "though I did hang out with her once at a party."

Sam didn't know what this meant, but thought it best not to pry. It was always best not to pry with Mike. Being around Mike was like being around a butterfly you'd come across in a field. Bright, beautiful, and perpetually inclined to fly away at any sudden, accidental movement.

Outside they sat on one of the cement benches that were built into the entrance of the school. Mike pulled his pack of cigarettes out and offered one to Sam. Sam took one. That was the thing about Mike, he was generous.

Mike leaned back and looked over at Sam and smiled. Sam smiled back. Mike took a long slow drag of his cigarette, turned around, and looked out at the mountains in front of the school.

"You ever go hiking?" He asked.

"Yeah," Sam said, turning and looking at the mountains. "I love that about living here. That, and the skiing. It's a good place."

"Yes, it is," Mike answered. "Sometimes I don't ever want to leave it. Sometimes I can't wait to get away." Sam nodded. He felt the same way. He worried about Cary. Her grades were terrible. She hated school and though she was graduating, she would have to do summer school to get her degree. She had talked about getting her GED and working, but Sam had convinced her to stay.

"Do you ever have ... strange thoughts?" Mike asked, his eyes going distant, foggy. Sam furrowed his brow.

"Like what kind of thoughts?"

"I don't know. Like, the kind of thoughts you're pretty sure no one else has." Mike looked up at the mountains again, and Sam watched the light on Mike's face.

"Sure."

They sat in silence for a time, Sam's mind running lose and terrible with curiosity. He knew better than to push Mike. And he also knew that Mike would say something much more interesting if he didn't.

"Have you heard of this thing called erotic asphyxiation?" Mike finally asked, lighting another cigarette and then pushing the lighter back into his jean pocket.

"Uh, no," Sam said honestly.

"Well, it's when you're having sex and the man chokes the woman, just a little."

Sam was shocked, though he tried desperately not to show it. "Why?" He asked, hoping his voice didn't sound too high.

Mike frowned as if the question was unimportant. "Well … I guess to make the sex better."

This seemed like a strange way to make sex better to Sam, as he couldn't imagine it any better than what he had with Cary.

"Huh," Sam said, "okay."

They were silent for a minute more, and then Sam asked, "Well, would the woman ever choke the man?"

Mike frowned again. "No, I don't think so." Mike took a deep drag and Sam felt confused. He didn't understand the purpose of anyone choking anyone, under any context and certainly not during sex. He couldn't imagine choking Cary; it in fact pained him to even think of it. Not to mention that she would probably kill him if he did.

"So Sam, could you give me a ride to the party? My vehicle is … indisposed at the moment." Mike chuckled.

"Sure. I can pick you up at eight?"

"Sounds good."

They sat smoking in silence, watching people pour out of the double doors, tidal in their motion. Sam looked over at Mike, who seemed to be watching everyone the way that one might watch a movie. He could even see the flat, strange reflection of all of their bodies in Mike's eyes.

* * *

"Good fucking God, Sam, why you always got to worry about me? I'll be fine. Something will work out," Cary said, shaking her head. They had ordered a large olive and mushroom pizza and were sitting at one of the wide wooden tables at Beau Jo's. Cary was wearing a tight red t-shirt and jeans, her eyes lined with black eyeliner.

"I'm sorry Cary. I just, you know ... think you're so smart, and–" here Cary cut him off.

"And what? I have to go to college to prove how fucking smart I am?"

Sam blinked, hard. And said nothing. Cary looked out the window and watched people walking by. The streets in Idaho Springs weren't particularly busy. It was mainly filled with townies, and a few folks on their way to the Ski Resorts. After a few minutes she shook her head, almost imperceptibly, and looked down at her plate.

"Look, Sam, I know ... you ... care about me. But, I just feel like, sometimes, well, you think that if I'm with you, I gotta be something I'm not. Like I gotta change into your mother or something to be good enough for you." She sat back and sighed.

Sam pulled his hand through his hair and thought. He always did that—never spoke before he thought. He knew that only led to you say something really stupid.

"I'm sorry I made you feel that way," he said after a few minutes. "I love you because of exactly who you are." She smiled a tight, thin line. He was the only one in their relationship who ever used the word love. She looked out the window again. And then back at Sam. She smiled and leaned over and pulled at the collar of his crisp, white t-shirt and said nothing. Sam smiled back. She leaned over and kissed him. He breathed her in and closed his eyes.

* * *

At Cary's house, they sat and watched TV with her father, Jim. He was a sweet, sad, white man in his early forties, but he looked like an old, old man to Sam. He had been in a terrible car accident not long after Cary's mother, who was Chickasaw, had left. Cary had told Sam that she didn't have any memories of her mother and that she didn't want any. And whenever Sam would try to broach the subject of knowing anything more about being Chickasaw, Cary would shut him down, fast.

It was always awkward watching television with Cary's father. He had suffered such intense neurological damage that he had trouble speaking and really never left his house. Sam had never seen him leave the couch, actually. He assumed that Cary was the only person in his life at this point. He would sit watching the television with child-like wonder, his hands folded in his lap, the ancient looking Pendleton that Cary was perpetually adjusting for him wrapped around his old, round shoulders.

They were watching an old black and white that Sam didn't recognize. He never seemed to be that particular about what was on, unless there was a lot of violence. Cary had told Sam that they would only have to sit with her father for a bit, before they partied. Sam didn't mind. It was uncomfortable, but Sam knew how much Cary loved her father, and he felt bad for him. It was terrifying to think that one tiny little moment in your life, one small decision would leave you your body, and take your soul.

"Daddy, do you want something to eat?" Cary asked. She was sitting next to him, leaning on him, rubbing his back. He shook his head no. "Daddy. I know you haven't eaten since I made you breakfast, and you hardly ate any of that. Come on

Dad, you have to eat, okay?" He turned to his daughter and smiled, his eyelids flickering as if he'd just turned towards a slight wind.

Sam got up and went to the kitchen. He made a sandwich with what was in the refrigerator, which wasn't much. Sam brought it out to Cary's dad and set it down in front of him and sat back down. He looked up at Sam briefly as he'd set the sandwich down, a look of mild confusion. He looked down at the sandwich of bologna and mayonnaise on white bread and wrinkled his nose.

"C'mon Daddy, just one bite."

He heaved his heavy shoulders and looked at Cary. She gave him a look of encouragement and he sighed and picked the sandwich up. He ate it and Cary watched him the whole way through. When he was done, Sam picked the plate up, went to the kitchen, and washed the plate. When he came back into the living room, Cary was standing and bending over to hug her dad. She finished, looked over at Sam, and smiled. He smiled back. Seeing her with her father reminded Sam of who Cary really was. It was part of why he loved her. He believed that he had seen that in her from the beginning.

"I'll be back later, Daddy," she said, and he looked up at her imploringly. "Cary," he said, and she walked back over to him, hugged him again, and headed back over to Sam, who was standing near the door.

"Bye, Daddy," she said, and before the door shut, he could see that Jim's gaze had returned to the TV, the light of it playing on his face, the shadows behind him making the whole thing look that much more eerie and sad.

Cary sighed heavily and looked over at Sam. "You don't have to do that, you know."

"My grandmother is like that. It's no big deal," he said; shrugging and taking her cold, copper colored hand. She looked down at their linked hands and silently put both of them over her heart.

* * *

Mike didn't understand why Sam was with Cary at all. He thought Cary loud, abrasive and as he had put it once to Sam, "ghetto," though Sam wondered if Mike had actually ever been to a ghetto, or really knew what that meant. Sam had cousins who lived in rough parts of Denver, and while Denver wasn't L.A., it could be rough on poor people. He knew that the parts of Denver where his cousins lived were probably considered ghettos to some, but Sam never felt weird, or unsafe or out of place there. Once a month, he and his mother would go visit his cousins and bring them food. Sometimes, one of his cousins would get in trouble, and he and his Mom would go down to the jail and bail them out, and take them home to their mothers.

On the few occasions that Mike had hung with Sam and Cary, it had been awful. Everything that came out of Cary's mouth had Mike rolling his eyes. And everything that came out of Mike's mouth had Cary doing the same. So, he wasn't really looking forward to going to a party with the both of them, though all three of them would have other friends there they could mix with, so, Sam hoped it wouldn't be too bad.

* * *

"He's a fucking dick, Sam. Why did we have to pick him up?"

This evening was going from worse to fucking terrible. Sam had delayed telling Cary about the fact that they had to pick Mike up until right before he was scheduled to do so, as he knew Cary would hate that he had agreed to pick him up and would try to convince him to leave him hanging. Honestly, Sam knew that Mike had probably just mentioned the party and encouraged him to come because he needed a ride, but Sam was just too nice to say no.

"Cary … " he said and she just rolled her eyes and went to join her friends, who were standing over in a corner, looking tough and wild with heavy black eyeliner and ripped up jeans. One of them was holding a bottle of Jack while the other leaned in front of her and let the first girl pour it down her throat. "Take it bitch!" one of the girls was saying, and they were all laughing.

As soon as Sam had pulled up in front of Mike earlier that evening, Mike had seen that Cary was in the car, and in the front seat and had sighed heavily and perceptibly before getting in the back of the old station wagon. As soon as he'd gotten in, he'd asked how Sam was, very pointedly ignoring Cary, at which Cary had said loudly, "And I'm *great*. Now that you're here." And laughed wildly. She had a six-pack of Budweiser up in the front of the car and picked one out of the plastic rings, twisting it free as if it were some kind of forbidden and lovely fruit. She knew that Sam hated it when she drank while either one of them drove. She had told him that she and her friends did it all the time and that they'd never gotten into trouble and that she knew all of the cops anyway.

Mike came sauntering up to Sam, a glass of something that looked like a gin and tonic in his hand, though Sam didn't recall seeing anything of that sort in the kitchen.

"Where'd your woman go?"

"She's in the corner." Sam gestured with his head in her direction and Mike looked for quite a while before looking back.

"She's out of control."

Sam laughed.

"What's so funny?" Mike said, sipping at his drink.

"Well, you like to do wild things. Why is it any different for you? Why should she behave any different?" He paused and then said, "I think she's strong."

Mike looked at Sam for a while, took another drink, and looked over again at Cary. Cary was now the one who was pouring Jack down a girl's throat and laughing wildly.

"That looks like strength to you? That looks like weakness to me. Look at her. Her friends. What do you think they'll be like in ten years? Come on Sam. Do you really think you and Cary will be on the same level in ten years? You're not on the same level now."

Sam closed his eyes on a pain that he couldn't voice. He couldn't stand the idea that life was like this, no matter how often it illustrated that it was. He looked over again and Cary was drinking from the bottle. She wasn't a big drinker, but when she did drink, she could handle her booze better than most.

"Besides. She makes herself vulnerable. All she does is show who she is, she broadcasts it like she doesn't care what the world can do to you. But it can fuck you over, and I know you know that. Especially when you're always showing it exactly where your weak spots are."

Sam frowned and looked down at his feet. He felt like crying. When he looked up, Mike was smiling. "Let's get you a G&T." He slung his arm around Sam and led him to the kitchen. "What's a G&T?" Sam asked and Mike laughed. "I like you," he answered.

They stood around for a while, socializing and talking with people. Every time Sam mentioned that he wanted to go over and check on Cary, Mike would tell him to let her be. Sam did think that he was being a *bit* of a doormat with Cary, though he couldn't imagine ever becoming anything like Mike. He figured he had to give her space and let her hang with her friends.

"So, I have a special treat for tonight. And I'm feeling pretty generous." Mike said. Mike's friends had wandered off after a long conversation about which kind of music they liked. It was interesting, Mike seemed to draw all kinds—they had talked to guys in football, track, guys who didn't play any kind of sport but they all seemed to have a basic respect for Mike.

"What's that?"

"Well, something I wonder if you've ever seen before. And … I want to share it with your girlfriend. I know I was too hard on her a bit ago. I know you really like her. I want all three of us to do it together."

"Sure," Sam said. He figured it was some high-grade weed. He rarely got high, and he hadn't gotten high for a while and it sounded kinda nice. He looked over at Mike, who had slung his long, brown arm around Sam again.

"I don't want to share it with anyone else," Mike said. "Let's go over to Cary and smoke some of the old peace pipe, shall we?" Sam laughed. Mike really wasn't a bad guy. They walked over to Cary and her group of friends, who eyed the both of them suspiciously. He couldn't imagine what they thought of him.

"Hey," Sam said softly.

"Hey," she said, smiling. Sam could tell that she wanted to be mad at him, but that she couldn't. She put both of her hands on her hips and mouthed *what?* at Sam and he laughed.

"So," Mike said, "I have something for the three of us."

"Oh, yeah?" She said sarcastically, her gaze shifting from Sam to Mike. Her eyes narrowed and her whole body stiffened.

"Really, it's something special and I wanted to share it with the two of you."

Cary eyed Mike suspiciously, and then looked over at Sam, who shrugged.

"What, heroin?" She asked.

Mike just laughed and then gestured with his head towards one of the bedrooms. Cary sighed loudly and said, "okay." She turned to her friends and said, "I'll be back."

They began walking towards the bedroom door that Mike had gestured towards, Mike leading the way. He knocked on the old wooden door once, gently, and then stuck his ear up to it. After a few seconds, he began to cautiously open the door. He peeked in and then swung the door wide open. Sam and Cary walked in, and Mike shut and locked the door. They sat down on the bed, which was unmade and covered in old blankets. The whole room was a mess—there were clothes everywhere, ashtrays overflowing with cigarettes, NASCAR posters up and in the spaces left, pictures of women in a series of compromising positions.

Sam tucked his hand into his jean pocket and brought out a little baggie full of white powder. Cary squealed. "Coke? Aw, fuck, I change my mind about you! You rock man," she said, giving Mike a brotherly punch on his arm.

Sam panicked. He felt a sharp, wild pain deep inside his gut. He did not want to do this. He didn't mind getting drunk, smoking weed once in a while, but … coke? This was just not him. He knew he had to draw a line somewhere.

"I don't know you guys …" he said, and Cary looked at him for a second and then shook her head. "Sam, for fuck's sake, it's only *coke*. It's not a big deal. And it's fun."

"Yeah, Sam, get over it, why don't you?"

Sam sat in silence for a few minutes, while Mike produced a small mirror, a tiny blade and a dollar bill, which he proceeded to roll up.

"Jesus, Sam, you can be such a killjoy," Cary said, looking over at Mike. Mike looked up from what he was doing and they two of them locked eyes and laughed. Sam felt terrible.

"C'mon, man, it's really no big deal. I've been doing coke for years, here and there—and I'm not addicted, if that's what you're thinking," Mike said, placing the mirror and small mound of coke on one of the old, wooden ancient looking nightstands. He had to brush a bunch of random objects away to make a space. He proceeded to cut the coke cleanly, and quickly.

"Whatever, man," Cary said, turning and sniffing a line, after taking the proffered rolled up bill. She sat up. "Ooh. That's good," she said, sniffing and wiping her nose.

Mike smiled. "Yeah. I only get the best. The best you can get here anyway." He and Cary laughed and Mike bent down and snorted a line. Mike shook his head a little, and then turned to Sam. "You know what? It's really no big deal. I hate it when people try to push me into something. I mean, that's stupid. Do what you want to do, I say."

Sam looked over at Cary who was looking at him in strange, exacting way. He'd never seen her look like that. Sam's head swirled. Cary blinked and then looked over at Mike and they locked eyes again and laughed.

"Gimmie that," Sam said, and opened his palm.

"You sure?" Mike asked, an amused expression on his face.

"Yeah." Sam took the rolled up bill from one of Mike's long, delicate hands and bent down to the mirror, his heart pounding. He sniffed through the tube, his nose burning. "Oh, jeez," he said and Cary and Mike laughed. Sam sat back. Almost immediately the world sharpened. He felt good.

"This isn't like weed at all," he said and Cary nodded. He was sure that Cary was looking at him with newfound respect. "I could stay up all night."

Mike looked at him and Sam was struck again by his beauty. He was like this perfect, impenetrable person. "You know I figure, why not try new things? Why not cross borders? What is life for anyway? We're all going to die someday. And we're really alone," Mike said, his dark dark eyes focused on Sam's.

"Yeah," Cary said. "People always leave."

Sam supposed this was all true. It didn't strike him as right exactly … but true. He wanted to hold Cary's hand, to tell her that he would never leave her, but he knew how she was. She would just laugh at him. Mike got up and went over to the old radio that was sitting on top of a chair in the corner. He pushed the clothes away that were draped over it with the back of his hand and pushed the on button. He turned the dial, the noises of the various stations floating in and just as quickly, out. Finally, he settled on a station, it's low, ominous sound floating out and into the room and making Sam feel strange, beautiful.

Mike came back to the bed and sat. He looked over at Cary, and then at Sam. "You two should dance." Cary laughed and then said, "okay." She pulled Sam up and Sam laughed as he tried to move around her. He was a terrible dancer. Mike laughed and started smoking. He watched them and Sam wondered what in hell had ever drawn Mike to him. Maybe because they were both Native? But there were a good handful of Natives in Clear Creek. But then again ... Mike wasn't friends with any of them. Or any of the Mexican students either. The only thing Sam could think was that maybe it was because they were two of the very few Natives in that school that lived a little outside of Idaho Springs, whose parents were college educated, middle class. Sam had seen Mike's parents once. They were clearly white. And Mike was very brown. And he didn't really look like a Native from North America ... but he didn't look Mexican either. Sam had never asked about any of this. He had just known not to.

"Why aren't you dancing?" Cary asked, looking at Mike.

"Because I don't dance."

"Well, clearly I don't either," Sam said and they all laughed.

Cary moved around Sam and he felt great. Everything felt sharper, clearer. He felt confident ... he felt like he had to pee. He stopped dancing.

"I'll be back," he said, kissing Cary's hand, walking past Mike, who was still watching Cary as she had kept on dancing.

He opened the door and shut it behind him and started walking through the crowd towards the bathroom. He was pretty sure he'd seen one not too long after he'd arrived. The lights were off, and someone had strung white Christmas lights around the house. Sam felt like soaring, like talking someone's head off about life, like dancing until he floated up to the white lights and disappeared. The party had gotten bigger, and pulsed with human activity, some people were on couches talking, some making out, and everywhere, people were dancing. It struck Sam like a bolt of lightning that this was beautiful. It was so hard to bear, the moment, that Sam had to stop for a moment, take a breath. He realized he was involuntarily holding his hand to his heart.

"Dude, get outta the fucking way!" A guy said, trying to get past Sam. Sam realized that he had stopped in the middle of the dancing crowd.

"Sorry," he said, the moment over.

He made his way over to the bathroom, which was miraculously empty, though in pretty sorry shape. He could see that though the partygoers had made it worse, it had more than obviously been a mess to begin with. The sink was covered in various tubes and bottles, their substances caking the basin. There were clothes strewn all over the incalculably dirty floor and an overflowing trashcan. He sighed and thanked God that he wasn't a woman, and didn't have to sit down on the toilet in front of him.

When he finished, he realized that he was already coming off his high. "That was quick," he said out loud. He felt like more. He closed his eyes and thought about what he had done, and why he'd done it. He sighed heavily and walked out of the bathroom, feeling funny, like he'd forgotten something.

Walking towards the bedroom, he realized what it was. He hadn't forgotten anything. He was remembering something. He pictured Cary dancing as he left the room, her eyes on Mike, his on hers. It was like a picture flashing in front of his face. He felt like his heart was being sharply pulled into his stomach. He began to run towards the bedroom. He stopped abruptly. He laughed. He had just tried coke for the first time and he was probably being paranoid. Wasn't that one of the effects?

He began walking again and unbidden, visions of Mike and Cary kissing passionately came to his mind, of them stroking each other's bodies, of Cary moaning like she never would with him. He felt torn, weirded out, and angry with himself. He kept walking.

At the door, he hesitated. He could go home right now. Just get in his car and drive home. Cary could get a ride home from one of her friends. And Mike had more friends at this party than most people have relatives. He sighed. That was wrong. His mother had taught him to be a good friend, always. He opened the door.

It was as if he was looking at one of his visions. There they were, fucking on the big, old bed they'd all been sharing just moments ago. He opened his mouth to scream at Cary, to call her a whore, when he blinked and saw that they were just sitting on the bed, talking. He felt crazy.

"Hey," Mike said, turning around. *Did he look funny?* "We thought we'd lost you there."

"Nah. Just had to get through the partiers," he said. He walked over to the two of them, and they'd obviously had more coke while he was in the bathroom.

"More?" Mike asked, proffering the mirror.

"No, thanks," Sam said and Mike shrugged and stared out the tiny, grimy window set in the wall in front of them. There were lights in the distance.

Cary turned to Sam. "You wanna go? I'm kinda tired suddenly, actually."

Sam was surprised. Usually, Cary was a real party animal and she'd just had a minimum of two snorts of coke.

"Sure," he said getting up from the bed. Cary got up too, and walked around the bed. Mike got up as well after scooping his mirror up from the nightstand, and they all walked towards the door, Sam leading.

Outside the party was still going pretty hard. Sam looked at his watch. It was two am.

"Well, you ready to go too?" Sam asked Mike.

"No," Mike said, "I can get a ride home. I think I want to hang some more. But, I'll see you at Track." He smiled. Sam smiled back. Sam noticed that Cary didn't say anything to Mike, but stared anxiously at the front door.

"Bye, Cary," Mike said, as soon as they'd turned to go. Sam looked back, but Mike had already disappeared into the crowd.

Sam shook his head, and took Cary's arm. They walked out together, Cary snatching a few beers in a brief detour to the kitchen.

They got in the car and Cary popped both beers open, and handed one to Sam. Normally, he'd object, but this time, he took it without question and drank deeply.

They were silent for a long time, Sam trying to work up the courage to ask her something, anything about Mike. The dirt road stretched out in front of them, and Sam could barely make out the forest on either side of the road, looking cool and ominous at this time of the night.

"So, what did you and Mike talk about while I was gone?"

Cary took a sharp breath and coughed a little, choking on her beer. "Nothing."

"What do you mean, nothing?"

Cary shook her head and looked out the window. "I mean, *nothing*." She sighed deeply. "He's really not that interesting." She pulled one of her long hands through her hair and closed her eyes. She opened them again after a few seconds, and looked again out the driver's side window, which was most of the way down.

"You ever notice how nice things smell at this time of the night?" She asked, her hair blowing back from the rush of air coming from the open window, her face still turned away from him. Sam was slightly taken aback. It was a very un-Cary like thing to say. Mike breathed in. It smelled like the forest, wind, dirt. It was a nice smell, even if it made him feel lonely too. He thought suddenly of his father, somewhere out there in the night. He pictured him as a beautiful, terrible thing. A man with hair like his, but blacker, and hands like his, but longer, more magical, strangers even to themselves. He knew that his father was in prison for helping someone to steal a train, and that he would be in prison for a long, long time. He sighed heavily and put his right hand on Cary's leg, and he could hear her exhale quietly, and jaggedly. She put her hand on his and his heart swelled with emotion for her, like an old car whose owner just kept flooding the engine, over and over, even when he knew he shouldn't.

A Smuggler's Atlas

Matthew Dexter

We loaded the canisters with dope and fired them across the moonlit desert into Arizona. Soup cans stuffed with cocaine capable of landing a thousand feet from the border. The canisters were colored to classify who launched them. We catapulted them into fields. If the Border Patrol discovered them floating on the Colorado River, someone was liable to lose an earlobe. The pneumatic cannon can misfire, errors were unavoidable.

We knew every constellation. We fired hundreds of kilos of cocaine into rotting saguaros. This was our sport—careers were bought and sold. Carbon dioxide tanks on our shoulders, blood vessels hardened by arteriosclerosis. It was better than chopping heads, or being ambushed by a sport utility vehicle pumping automatic weapons, or throwing a Molotov cocktail into an Acapulco nightclub.

Brush up to our shoulders; we were close enough to launch loogies at the border fence. Our fingers blistered, knuckles purple, puss poured from calluses. We did this every night with the gringo farmer. We aimed for his fields.

When the work was done and our muscles were aching, we drove home, waving to the Policía with our giant rusty cannon reflecting the rising sun, a decadent middle finger to the Border Patrol. The whole village watched us; most residents too poor for vehicles. Our neighbors despised us and grinned through clenched incisors.

Sixty percent of the cocaine that passes into Arizona goes through our town, our tunnel. Smugglers stay overnight while waiting for clandestine vehicles to load with invisible marching powder for other parts of the border.

During the seasonal debauch, samples of unlimited products are provided for all to enjoy. The people get so wired when the smugglers leave town that they start building elaborate makeshift houses made out of plywood and tarps, but then the drugs wear off and the houses are in worse shape than before.

* * *

It is the unkempt roadside crosses that attract me most: those beneath murderous curves, twisted guardrails, mangled vehicles moaning in the wind. They drive with broken headlights, charred vehicles rusting for decades, or disintegrated. The fatalities are seldom innocent; drivers are often struck by fortunate cows. The corpses who wear seatbelts are melted until the Bomberos carry plastic plates with barbecue onto the truck, reeking of mesquite and alcohol.

There are hundreds of kilometers with no Bomberos, no hospitals—no hope. Call a tow truck from a tiny village and drag up the body. Many plummets go unreported. The invisible islands of the night—where spirits whisper melodies as sirens careening from the *carreterra* with a vehicle full of beer cans.

My headlights reflect the roadside *Cuervo Peligroso* warnings: Dangerous Curves. I always pray after midnight, when only the most insane of ageless truck drivers are plowing through the mountains—tires nudging the ledge, decapitating rabbits, tossing gravel toward corpses, roaring rigs covered with graffiti coiling around the narrow starlit abysses with the wisdom of chariot-donning warriors returning from the afterworld.

The *carreterra* is tight near shrines. I must park kilometers away then hike upward or downward toward the scene of the beautiful death: plummeting through the scenery of a postcard, that final moment floating into the ethereal landscape of dazzle—mesmerized by wind rippling through exploding eardrums with beer cans rattling against the roof of a cavern. Careening from the *carreterra* into shards of twisted steel, moaning to a cathedral speckled upon the pebbles and boulders for vultures to worship.

I park next to the abandoned farm where bandits siphon gasoline from a rusty barrel to tourists unaware of the distance between *gasolineras*. The bastards do not bother me or my Toyota. Bandits respect these memorials. I wipe my sweat with a towel before kneeling next to the altar. I clean the debris from the wooden crosses and the spider webs from the abandoned candles. I light their wicks, place fresh flowers, and clear the dead foliage and garbage thrown from vehicles. I walk down that cavern toward the cars and pick the neglected possessions from the remnants. There is always something new.

When the vehicles are in decent shape, I crawl inside and listen to the echoes of the dying, my knuckles massaging the rust and coarse defecations adorning charred chariots; but at this particular curve, nothing is able to withstand the jagged boulders which mark the entry to the butterfly-strewn desert.

* * *

The tunnel connecting San Ysidro to Tijuana traverses three miles and costs more money than any drug tunnel ever built. It never ends. We supervise teenagers loading robotic wagons. The bottom is magnetic and it glides like an airport passenger between gates. The electronic floor is so shiny that it glimmers through the thickest of human eyelids. The passage is illuminated with bulbs that never die, and nobody knows how long the tunnel has existed. None of the employees remember its construction. The sophistication is well beyond the mediocre structures of the Border Patrol checkpoints and their flimsy fence, which the tunnel passes through at no less than six different intervals.

My uncle lives in one of those houses on the other side and sometimes we dig into the bedrooms of relatives. The cartels need every passage they can get. We have no idea how many exist. We follow our routes. We digest dinner as green and white Border Patrol vehicles cruise the street out front. We wave when they watch us through the windows, with warm tortillas in our mouths.

We have many wounds. My wrists and forearms are scarred from the casino fire. We could hear the slot machines and the muffled chorus of screaming patrons asphyxiating in bathrooms waiting for their faces to melt. We shouted for them to leave before igniting the gasoline, but some proceeded to the back, presuming there was an unlocked exit—there was not. We filled the front with flames. I dragged two waitresses to safety. I saw my face in the flames, and later in the bricks of cocaine, sculpted with such glory and precision.

* * *

Your first gunfight makes you a man, whether you die in a pool of blood beside the passenger door of a Pathfinder, or survive to spit bullets from automatic weapons another day. My grandfather was involved in my first gunfight. *Balacera* is what we Mexicans refer to as a gunfight. Gringos sometimes think of gunfights as western style shootouts with cowboys fingering leather holsters. It is nothing of the sort. It is combat without military gear. Cars and houses and bodies are riddled with bullets. Three minutes go by like the flash of a firefly landing on your Adam's apple.

Grandpa was hit in the throat during the seventh minute. He prayed that the teenagers would be able to slay him painlessly. A stub of the toe and Grandpa would wince and sulk in his bedroom for hours. Grandpa was not killed fast. He slumped over the hood of the Pathfinder, clutching the gaping wound, mumbling amid the gunfire.

My brother charged the vehicle we ambushed, assassinated the driver to the drone of barking dogs. Humans never speak after a good gunfight. I carried Grandpa on my shoulders until he grew heavy. The grass swallowed him as ambulances and police vehicles engulfed us.

My brother hanged himself in his holding cell with his cowboy belt. The buckle was embedded into his throat in the same spot where Grandpa was shot. I punched the walls till my knuckles bled and disappeared. A year later, rolled out of prison in a laundry truck filled with feces and urine.

* * *

I was ambushed in the rental car when my son was sleeping in the backseat. The boy was blasted through his skull. But it did not kill him—only made him speak sentences backwards and pump bullets with venom. This instance turned the boy into a savage and word has it he decapitated fifty foot soldiers of Las Zetas before being flayed alive. That is no easy task, let me tell you. This is a family affair.

* * *

The procession of vehicles waiting to make it through the Border Patrol checkpoint into San Diego meanders its way through children soiled with filth who peddle trinkets with yellow teeth. Their parents wave water bottles and refreshments in the air above anemic skulls. The women get so close to the car that you can see their armpit hair. The abnormally long one leads the way. It curls itself around the window and threatens to enter. This black coarse reminder of what life would be without the cartels tucks itself on the tinted edge of the window, my thumb on the button to make it disappear. They are nothing without us: these children. No different than the kids and adults on the other side of the border. We are modern-day saviors who risk our lives every second to deliver the shipments that provide the medicine that Americans need. Without people like me, the prices would skyrocket. The cars coil into rattlesnakes and you can hear the instruments and the children sitting on the dashboard of the affluent, wiping windshield with spit. I nod, safe behind sunglasses.

They tug on my wipers, swipe the glass with hairless elbows. The children would give anything to be on that other side of the border. I shove one of them into the trunk. Two others force themselves inside and we race toward the Gringos with their machine guns aimed at my face. I hit the brakes and skid marks fill my shorts. They drag me from the vehicle. You can hear the children banging on the trunk, begging for America.

The kids are freed and escorted back across the border—but they run—fast as their sandals will allow—these illegal immigrants sprinting toward paradise, chased by Border Patrol agents to the sound of honking horns in honor. Delighted, some Mexicans shout *órale* from their windows. Sweaty men with no air condition in their trucks pump their fists. Knuckles are the exuberance of a new nation, one where detainment never matters. The cars celebrate these young pedestrians with no chance of escaping.

The residual odor in my trunk attracts dogs and the agents lead me into their decrepit office—nothing compared to the house of a smuggler.

"You speak English?" they ask.

The men have Mexican accents as thick as my parents'. Their skin is darker than mine, and their arms are the same length as my dead sister's. There is not much difference in our heritage. Our genitals are the same. Except my balls are bigger, larger than you have ever seen, and the measurements are something that prison guards can confirm should anybody desire to track them down.

"English is my language," I tell them.

They nod and lick their lips.

"Hope those goddamn wetbacks get some food and water before they return to the squalor," I say.

"What is your citizenship?" the agent asks.

I tell them the truth. There is nothing left to die for. Smuggling is a business and the bastards will breathe into your eyelashes with wicked odor. I tell myself (in English) to remain calm: *You are detained by Gringos. Their wall is nothing. People are crawling through it as we speak.*

* * *

My instructions were to strangle my attorney. Guys like me always get the best lawyers. He sat across from me in the holding cell, my legs shackled to the table to prevent a repeat of my tantrum that caused the concussion of two other inmates and the broken nose of an inhospitable guard.

My attorney told me that Las Zetas targeted his daughter for getting men like me acquitted. He drove around in a bulletproof Hummer to the tunes of Mozart, smoking cigars down to his fingers and then digging them into the ashes of the cup holder. He said they tortured her naked and hung her from a bridge in Acapulco during spring break.

His daughter was merely doing beer bongs and flashing her mosquito bites. He told me that when he went down to identify the body—protected by thugs and goons paid twice his salary—her nipples were branded with warnings and her stomach was carved with a *Z*. Her fingertips were amputated and they decapitated her and put the video on YouTube.

It didn't matter; I had to kill him. My bosses had hired me for similar jobs with local Policía. This was my mission. The fireflies in his eyes and the wrinkles of his forehead warned me to abandon the idea. The poor soul was the same as me. I warned my attorney about the hit. I told the government everything they asked to avoid trial.

* * *

I wanted them to send me to some exotic country. Somewhere warm with monkeys jumping from banana trees and parrots to keep me company. They refused. I told them someplace with tacos and saguaros and mariachi, but ended up in Wisconsin with a common gringo name and a damn white picket fence covered in snowflakes. This was the first time I lived in a cold climate and it fit me this old house by myself. I sat by the chimney, drinking tequila, burning pieces of the basement that I chopped with my axe. I waited for the cartel to bust down the door, and got fat from all the deer meat in my freezer.

Bambi was delivered by my amicable neighbor. He got me out of the house with the allure of smoking crystal and slaughtering animals during hunting trips. We killed bears and moose. It was no different than shooting thugs and gangbangers. It felt nice to bring down a beast bigger than El Chapo. But I was addicted to the pipe. The Program knew this and flew me out to a clinic for six weeks under the guise of visiting a dying aunt. The day after my return the neighbor was dead. Not from meth, but from a baby bear which tore into his bedroom in the middle of the night. He had a heart attack when the things started snuggling beneath the sheets.

The bear was hunted. The man was wheeled from his house. The animal was slaughtered and fallen from its branches, its face so tortured and surprised that it exuded the expression of a hirsute obese hunter. The authorities dragged the bear to a caged truck and tossed its corpse inside. The snow had some puddles of bear blood; and when I was alone I smothered myself in the viscous *sangre* and filled my house with smoke. I opened the door so the bear's mother would come inside.

* * *

After recovering from the mauling, the agents stuck me in the same house.

"You are one of America's Most Wanted," said the bear.

The animal would sit on the steps out front with the door barricaded with planks. There was nothing left of the basement; that is where I began sleeping after the deer returned and began creeping down the snow to peek into my windows while I dreamt. They darting away into the brush—these beatific creatures which once satisfied me so much. They started watching me in the kitchen. The snow covered the bottom half of the windows, but then it melted and the glass was covered in animal hides which attracted maggots and ants, but this did not bother me.

"What have you come for?" the bear asked.

Each day the bear grew wiser and larger and no longer was I afraid of her. I killed the deer that dashed through the glass window that cast no reflection. The ones who were not fatally injured were stitched up and given their rightful place at the dinner table. The bear did not return for months. Then the basement was shaking and the bear wrestled itself down the staircase. I was sure the animal had come to snuggle.

I was wrong. It took my eyes and strung them from the corners of the sockets for a second before slicing them with its claws. The deer did not offer assistance. The animal was serene after it disappeared, and sensing my ineptitude began to moan and cuddle on the filthy mattress filled with blood.

"This is your last chance to make a change," the bear said.

The animal was capable of keeping me warm. It dragged me up the broken stairs and placed me on the shredded leather couch soiled by deer defecations. The beast seemed to push the hard briskets of feces and mud aside and shoved me into a pocket. The bear pulled me toward the fire, the legless couch dragging itself in victory against the bloodstained floorboards.

She positioned me near enough to keep warm without being close enough to burn. The hot putrid air of breath as it passed in exasperation through those moist motherly nostrils was a comfort I hadn't experienced since winning my first *balacera*. The snout with its whiskers tickling my neck made the pain diminish, but agony was what I had been missing in my life. It felt nice to be blind with the bear gnawing on food from the refrigerator.

She poured me a glass of whiskey and made sure I knew where the bottle was kept, and its distance was measured by my fingers no less than seven occasions to assure me that the Jameson was located in an ideal spot. She was loquacious and spoke elegantly about many topics that had never occurred to me.

The mahogany of the mantle was placed over my shoulders and stomped into dozens of pieces of wood for the fire. These were laid on my lap and beside my feet as the bear retreated into the woods.

* * *

I waited for the bear to return, but she never did. I spent all my time thinking about the things she said. I would tell her how things could be clearer with no eyeballs than the ice melting into my warm glass of whiskey. I had managed to crawl to the liquor cabinet and kept alive on the rotting carcasses of deer meat covered with maggots. Flies swarmed my eye sockets, so I covered them with a blanket and waited for the bear to show.

* * *

The agents shook me and their voices came through the stupor like lightning in the fog. They placed me in a hospital, and pumped me full of drugs and nutrients. The sweet nurse bathed me and shaved my face when I wanted to feel like a man again—not just some animal.

There wasn't much for me to hope for and The United States Federal Witness Protection Program could only carry me so far. They were convinced that I was insane, suicidal, and a threat to the men and women who kept visiting me at the hospital, offering their condolences and bloating me with chocolate. I fingered the balloons full of helium. They had to keep me protected, safe from those who wanted to castrate me and hang my headless corpse from an American bridge glimmering with steel.

There was still beauty in the world. More so than ever; the good of the planet crossing spheres could be sensed with tunnel vision and the dying souls entered my room through the vents at the top of the wall where the warm air kept us alive. I was able to take the pulse of the hospital with my nostrils, and one night when there was a thunderstorm so loud that human voices melted into nothingness, at last, I entered the elevator shaft with gusto and walked out the front door of the hospital.

* * *

Good thing about being blind was that the cartels would never expect it. So they shipped me out west, gave me another gringo name even more common, but this time they rented me a cheap one-bedroom apartment on Silverbell Road. It was decent. The small space was easy to manage, and I was able to dance around the furniture. Without sight, it is not necessary to have so much space. People do not realize this until they die, when the walls close in.

I took up golf and became popular at the driving range. I would hit the course with the men as their guest. They let me drive the cart across the fairways, and I floored the plastic peddle into the rubber beneath my cleats. One day I kept going, my Titleist gloves gripping the wheel with white knuckles—we catapulted the cart into the center of a sand trap. The guys laughed it off and let me to drive my own cart after that. I had memorized the course to a tee and indeed the University of Arizona campus could be maneuvered with ease. Within months, I had become a respected civilian, admired by affluent Gringos. They would sit in my ratty apartment and mingle.

Another activity I enjoyed was hanging around the nudist colony where one of my foursome worked as accountant. I was able to massage suntan lotion on the backs of the ladies who kept me company by the pool. The odor of jasmine borne by the desert, the giggles of the cougars, and groans of the old men who offered my cocktails, was the perfect accompaniment to the chirping of robins and the drone of bumblebees.

I was the envy of the country club and all men looked up to me, especially in the men's room, where I spent a great deal of time handing out fancy towels. I mesmerized them with my blue comb swimming in a jar of Barbicide. Dipping my wand into the cauldron, they would offer generous tips and enjoyed their minutes away from their wives or golf buddies. They shared their innermost secrets, and I knew who they were by the splash of piss against the urinal cake or the sound of gas emitted between expulsions in sparkling porcelain tanks secluded by smooth mahogany.

There was no monotony to their movements, and my life was perfect. For the first time, there were no worries about dying, or seeing into the future. The bear had given me the gift of illumination and the Witness Protection Program had turned me into a superhero. Every morning, a different woman from the country club would drive her husband's foreign car into Silverwood Terrace Apartments to fuck me on my grimy futon. Punks would smash their car windows with rocks and steal the pocketbooks and stereos. I told these ladies to take taxis, warned them of the vandals, but they ladies refused to listen, until they heard the echo of shattering glass during doggy style.

* * *

Silverbell Terrace was not a ghetto. It was indeed a decent place for college students and the working poor, conveniently situated three miles northwest of the University of Arizona, just about where the city merges into desert and dirt roads. Silverbell Terrace had the maintenance man and gardeners. It had the cocaine cowboys and alcoholics. The grass was green. The pool was kept in pristine condition and the palm fronds were prevented from resting downward dead and depressed like many residents.

Many renters were ambitious. Some were heavy sleepers. The police helicopters were pervasive. The spotlights penetrated through the tapestries and curtains and duct tape and aluminum foil. The inertia of the rotors was so powerful that the dead flowers from my stolen trees bounced back and forth across the terrace in front of the door to my apartment.

You could hear a hundred toilets flushing at the same time; frantic fiends flushing their deviance down the shitter. I stole the trees from ABCO Desert Market after grocery shopping. Nobody ever suspects a blind man. Truth is that the police helicopter only arrived for armed robberies, usually at the ABCO. They do not come for stolen plants.

After morning sex, I pretended to read the latest issue of *Penthouse* in a chaise longue next to the swimming pool. I am ashamed of my nipples and my body. I never removed my t-shirt in public, and therefore had a perpetual farmer's tan and the manager whispered as she passed through the gates from her office to the paths that lead through meandering cacti and palm trees to the turquoise and tan apartments. I never wore sunscreen. My skin meant nothing to me. I collected hyperpigmented dots and brown freckles to prove the illusion that I was human.

The Mexican maintenance man never formally introduced himself—but he smiled and tossed marijuana grenades at my feet whenever he saw me walking. I clutched the plastic bags and pocketed them. He was a generous saint. I imagine he must have discovered ounces while cleaning out apartments. The tenants would snort the couches if possible. I found a fat rock of cocaine wrapped in a wad of *The Tucson Daily Star* in my rented couch the first week I moved in. Hours were wasting blowing this stellar rock and moving furniture, hanging speaker wires, and tweaking alone till a few hours before dawn. There must have been nearly a hundred dollars of Indian reservation marching powder.

Al was a Mexican ex-convict who lived on the second floor of the corner apartment closest to the south side of the parking lot, right above Jon Enriquez and his mother, the latter of whom had a tendency to peek out the windows at the pedestrians and pontificate all the rumors and truths despite her inability to speak a word of English.

We all had four units to our building and Silverwood Terrace was full of degenerates and vile individuals. This is not to say that there were not some decent people in the complex, but our four or five clustered buildings consisted of despicable hearts in at least a couple apartments and all of us had issues, even the girls who lived with kittens and the old men with tinfoil on their windows.

Cocaine was in most of those apartments. Weed was smoked by almost all of us and it was a neighborly miracle a few months after I moved in when I noticed four generations of degenerates, many of whom had never spoken to each other, establishing a crescendo of interactions and drug deals centered around the grass and asphalt and palm trees.

When I say that there were good people of lower income in the apartments—amid the criminals, dealers, users, students—there were Mexicans and poor families that were forced to live among us, and their children would ride rusty bikes and fly kites made from materials in Mom's kitchen with grimy fingers. The parents might have been great people, but their children taunted me. One especially loquacious seven-year-old would say: "You think you're sooooo cool…you think you're so cool."

I was six times his age, twice his height, and he chopped me down to the size of fire ants scurrying across Slushies. Everybody encouraged the incessant chants and smirk of this future cartel member. My adulterers were powerless to the pure visceral comedy of this little punk putting me in my place. I had to take it. Nodding my head like a dysfunctional narcoleptic turkey, bobbing to the rhythms of sadistic laughter from an eight-year-old bully.

* * *

The dichotomy between the country club people and my fellow residents of Silverbell Terrace could not have been clearer. Their voices, odors, vocabulary, styles of debauchery; I was a blind man trapped between two opposite worlds. And then, the boy was duct-taped to my bed, sweating into the pillowcase.

I carved flesh from his kneecaps and elbows and the tip of his nose, to the melody of birds beating their beaks against the window. I flayed him as I had done with members of the Gulf Cartel so many times. This boy who had made a mockery of me was remorseful.

No longer protected by the Gringos, I fled to Mexico, aware that there was no turning back, no way to avoid being tracked. It was only a matter of time. Still, I kept a low profile and rented a hut on the beach in Oaxaca. I had money saved, but knew that I would not need it.

Paranoia spun sandy moonlight from howling animals. I was unable to sleep. I spent most my waking energy collecting driftwood. The monkeys were plotting and soon they would attack. The skirmishes were a daily occurrence. They would pounce with the numbers to slaughter me in the depths of slumber. I was building a raft to sail into the Pacific.

* * *

My vessel was built by the fingers of a blind man and I had no way of ascertaining the craftsmanship. I half-expected the thing to sink soon after getting past the breakers that kept knocking me into the foam. My ankle was attached to the raft by knotted monkey tails. After an hour, things grew calm and I covered myself in the Mexican blanket to protect my skin from the sun. I survived on tropical fish captured by lucky thrusts of a sharpened driftwood spear. I was able to warm the catch in the sun for an hour, wrestling pelicans the first few days, until they disappeared.

I starved for days and started eating the monkey tails until there was nothing left to connect me to the raft. One morning, the horn of the Carnival Elation knocked me into the waves borne by the ship. The reverberation was so loud that I could hear it beneath the surface, and grew convinced the ship was going to swallow me. I lost my raft. I could sense the shadow looming over me, shading me from the sun. My flesh was cold with the breeze. Men with Australian accents pulled me aboard a shuttle boat which journeyed toward an enormous debauch. I was welcomed with margaritas, music, and applause on the sundeck of the Carnival Elation. The people reeked of suntan lotion, alcohol, and the aroma of gourmet food was clinging to the fluffy towels they wrapped me with. The salt on the rim tasted like the ocean and there was nothing between me and these Caucasian cruisers with their obsession for shuffleboard, buffet decadence, and driving golf balls off the upper deck.

One night after midnight brunch, upon overhearing about the moonlit beauty of the Baja, I excused myself to the bathroom and jumped off the eighth deck of the Carnival Elation. Cracked my skull against the ship but kept my cool as the water engulfed me and swam as the blood poured from my wound. The waves pushed me toward the shore, muscles driven by the inertia of a suicide jumper's mind in midair. It was difficult to measure the distance between me and the bottom of the cruise ship. This was not an Acapulco cliff dive. This was the first time my blind prescience had gone awry.

The waves knocked me against the corral and I knew it was the end. But something in the back of my head poured into my nostrils and I climbed the corral. The crabs scattered as I crawled. Sea urchins stabbed my kneecaps and elbows. Rolling into puddles, crabs pinched my hands and face. The tides would wash over me and bring more puddles, but I could measure the distance to the edges of this promontory by the sound of the waves on every side. I kept going till I could feel sand in the bottom of the puddles. When I arrived at the beach, I tossed my bloodied body into the waves and let the sea roll me back and forth.

When I woke to the rising tide the air was cool and the sounds of birds engulfed the canopies of trees. My skin was raw and through my eyelids I caught visions of the dead skinless boy. I could see his face perfect before the savage act. From the job I did with the flaying, I was able to trace the scars and wrinkles and dimples and moles which littered his flesh. In my eyelids he approached and asked for forgiveness. I could not grant him that.

Monkeys came down from the trees. My dream from the start: to get rich and live off the work of the monkeys, their nimble fingers delivering dinners prone to cause diarrhea. It was a perfect system. We would lounge in hammocks and get lost in the horizon. These monkeys did not see things as I did. They began slapping my wounds and rubbing my skull. They ripped the clothing from my skin.

The monkeys threw feces at me, hobbled away, and here they left my bloodied body naked except for the golf ball that had been lodged in the back pocket of the trousers I had borrowed from one of the omelet chefs who befriended me at sea. I rubbed the craters on the Titleist as the moon rose higher and swallowed the sand in an attempt to choke, but the monkeys returned and cleaned out my windpipes. They kept me warm as I wept, and together our voices merged into the ocean.

* * *

The rain soaked the island every afternoon. The palm trees were very tall and I was only able to climb a couple because they had many twists and turns where hurricanes had blown them horizontal. Each morning I walked the perimeter: a short distance of perfect sand interrupted by the corral outcropping. I plucked sand dollars with my toes and laid starfish for my bed and pillow. Each day I would collect a new batch. I sharpened driftwood on stones until the wood was burning and stabbed my kneecaps, elbows, and earlobes—peeling the flesh and then ripping the cartilage from my nose with my fingernails.

The coconuts were so sparse that the monkeys fought for them and attempted to steal the chunks of smashed fruit. They would disappear to their trees and I would chuck rocks at the tops, hoping to hit a wayward coconut. When one landed, the monkeys would take it, but I would wrestle with great hunger over the coconut before they were able to escape with it. They bit pieces of my flesh and these gangrene chunks were flayed off beneath the rain. But then the coconuts ran out. The monkeys stayed in their trees, and once in a while they would fight for food and one would drop to its death against the corral.

They left me to die. I would sit out in the sun, flaying pieces of my face, ripping out chunks of hair. I wanted to drown. The monkeys would return to earth to eat their murdered counterparts, and I would wrestle them for scraps, and my arms and legs and everywhere bore the mark of their teeth. I chopped their tails and ate them raw as the monkeys squirmed in

anguish. Soon there were no more monkeys. I scattered the island searching for their carcasses before the savage birds would
come down or the waves would carry the fallen monkeys to
their watery graves.

The birds started dropping from the sky. I ate them raw and
survived on the nutrients of dead fish washed ashore. Then the
rains stopped. Everything stopped and there was no life on the
island outside of my own skinless body. I started peeling the
skin from my left foot, then the ankle, and kneecap, and hip.
Soon there was no skin from the soles of my feet to the rim of
my penis. My waist went next, followed by my torso, shoulders,
back, and delicious buttocks. My arms and hands were fantastic, but then things got difficult. The neck was much more
complicated, and it got to the point where there was nothing
left of my body. That is when I cut off my tongue. Insects were
oppressive. They rose from my skin when I slept. I kept myself
in the ocean all day. When the sailboat arrived, I was doing the
dead man's float when the wife called out.

"Another cartel killing," said a man's voice.

I could hear the wife vomiting into the ocean.

"Turn away, Gary, please," she said.

The man growled and I rolled over, again and again until the
woman was screaming and the man was cursing at me to grab
the rope. I screamed that I was blind, but he did not understand what I was saying and then when he sailed closer he saw
that my tongue was missing.

"Jesus Christ, mate!"

"What the hell happened to you?"

"Who did this?"

I told them everything, but the words were atavistic, not
human. The man pulled me aboard and the wife cried. I could
hear them talking about what to do with me. I had not moved
in hours. They pontificated about infectious diseases.

"What the hell are these animals?" the wife asked.

The man groaned. He placed his ear against where my lips used to be and bubbles erupted from my mouth to assure him I was still alive. He tossed me into the water.

* * *

I began to grow new skin. Not everywhere, and not of the same texture as before, but the salt water and air seemed to help. The couple dropped me in the breakwater of the island where they found me floating, and the waves welcomed me to shore. There was no escaping my own skin, and it grew crusty and soon I was attached to the corral. I lay there in the sun and waited for the rains which never came, and the days floated into one. The engine of the cartel boat was an aberration, I was certain.

Voices from the Grand Jury

Julian Berengaut

Manager of grand jury operations to jurors during the orientation

"You can take notes but don't ask me for more writing paper. The more paper I buy, the more people use it."

* * *

2nd Degree Murder while Armed (drug deal gone sour)

Juror to witness (mother of victim): What was the fence in your backyard made of? Metal, wood?

Assistant US Attorney (AUSA) to the juror: I don't see how that is relevant. You have heard testimony that the shooter shot the victim over the fence.

* * *

2nd Degree Burglary, Theft, Receiving Stolen Property, Obstruction of Justice

AUSA to victim

"What was taken from the apartment?"
"Two flat screen TVs."
"What else?"
"An air conditioner."
"Anything else?"

"My daughter's toys."
"Anything else?"
"Dishes and place mats."
"Anything else?"
"Food from the refrigerator."
"Food from the refrigerator?"
"Yeah, hamburger meat."

* * *

Juror (white, elderly, upper crust lady) to witness

"Now, what did you think she meant when she said to you: 'Bitch, I'm gonna fuck you up'?"

* * *

AUSA, an attractive young woman, to the jury: Are there any questions for me about this case?
Juror, another attractive young woman: Yes, I have a question, where did you buy your shoes?

* * *

Assault with Intent to Rob (street crime)

AUSA to victim

"When the man came up to you, did he say anything?"
"He told me to give him my purse."
"What were the exact words that he used?"
"Bitch, give me the fucking purse."

* * *

Grand jury foreperson swearing-in a witness brought from jail, in handcuffs and leg irons

"Raise your right hand ... well, as far as you are able."

* * *

Assault with Deadly Weapon *(fight during a barbeque in a public park over a woman flirting)*

AUSA to witness

"Was there a fight?"

"Yes, the two women who had words started to fight."

"Fighting how?"

"Pulling hair and punching."

"What happened then?"

"The two men pulled them apart."

"Did the defendant's girlfriend do anything at that time?"

"Yeah. She didn't want the fight to end."

"Did she say anything?"

"Fuck that bitch up."

* * *

AUSA to witness

"Have you ever dated the defendant?"

"I don't consider it dating—we had sex."

* * *

AUSA to witness

"Have you ever been convicted of any crime"?

"They said I did welfare fraud."

"But was there a conviction?"

"I don't know. They made me pay back the check."

* * *

Juror to her fellow jurors, apropos of nothing, during break

"I only go to McDonald's when I'm hung over, and I don't have a hangover today."

* * *

1st Degree Burglary While Armed

Juror to victim

"You said that the defendant was making jabbing motions with a shiny object?"

"Yes."

"Was the shiny object she had in her hand big or small?"

Victim looks at juror as if he is a complete moron.

"Big enough for me to get scared and back away."

* * *

1st Degree Burglary While Armed

AUSA to victim

"Were you at home in the morning on June 17?"

"Yes."

"Did anything happen?"

"Yes."

"Could you describe what happened?"

"I went back to sleep after my wife left for work."

"What time was that?"

"6 AM."

"Did you talk to your wife?"

"Yes. I asked her to leave me two cigarettes."

"And then you fell asleep?"

"Yes."

"What woke you up?"

"There was a lady next to my bed."

"What did you do?"

"I screamed."

"What did you scream?"

"Get away from me! I have a wife! How did you get in here?"

"And did the lady say anything?"

"Yes."

"What did she say?"

"Give me your money or I'll hurt you."

"And then what did she do?"

"She waved what looked like a black sock."

"What there anything special about the black sock."

"Yes. It had a rock in it."

* * *

AUSA to the victim's partner

"Who do you live with?"

"I live with my fiancé."

"How long have you lived with him?"

"Twenty-six years."

* * *

1st **Degree Murder** *(attempted drug robbery)*

Juror to witness

"What did you do when you heard the shots?"

"The shots? You don't pay attention to shots. You hear them all the time. If you are in bed, you stay in bed, if you watch TV, you continue to watch TV—but you keep your head down."

* * *

Juror to witness

"I am confused. Your girlfriend was Shawn?"

"Yes."

"So who were Gloria and Marilyn?"

"Well, as it was presented to me, Gloria was Shawn's friend and Marilyn lived nearby."

"You also said that someone was turning tricks for drugs. Who was that?"

"Well, Marilyn ... and Gloria ... and Shawn and pretty much every woman living in that neighborhood."

* * *

Double Murder *(revenge shooting following a robbery)*

AUSA to witness

"What did you do when you heard the shots?"
"I lay down on the floor."
"And then what did you do?"
"I tried to get under the bed."

AUSA to witness (regarding location of houses)

"Do you know what 'perpendicular' means?"
"No."

* * *

Involuntary Manslaughter *(drunk driving)*

Witness (victim's friend)

"Yeah. He was concerned as well, I mean, because, you know, the deal was that I will be talking or whatever, and then he is like yo, and he's like well, whatever, so he started doing his little flirting thing or whatever, and I noticed this time, I'm like yo, I don't see her, so, you know, Shawn, go look in the bathroom, make sure she is good."

Witness (another friend)

"I know this time from that I'm definitely taking the keys from somebody. I don't care if I have to beat them up, you know. It's just like send me to jail for the night for beating you up and throwing your keys in the gutter, but at least I know in my heart this person didn't die tonight or the people in the car. This hits pretty hard. I was the last dude to kiss that girl."

* * *

Robbery *(high school senior on the way from school to his girlfriend's house)*

AUSA to victim

"What did they take from you?"
"My wallet"
"What was in you wallet?"
"My debit card."
"How much did you have on your debit card?"
"40 dollars."
"What else did they take?"
"My shoes."
"Your shoes?"
"Yes. My shoes."

* * *

AUSA to witness (victim's girlfriend)

"Are you here voluntarily?
"… No."
"Let me rephrase that. Has anyone forced you to come here?"
"Oh, no."

* * *

Assault with Dangerous Weapon *(feud of two families living in neighboring row houses)*

AUSA to witness:

"Were there any threats?
"It was constant: that bitch this, that bitch that, I don't like them bitches living over there."
"Any other?"
"Yeah. I heard them say they can't burn our house down because their own house gonna catch fire."

* * *

Aggravated Assault (*fistfight following club closing*)

AUSA to witness (friend of victim)

"Were you concerned when you were approached by the defendant and his friends?"

"No, I wasn't."

"Why?"

"Because Kevin was with us. He is always very friendly and he knows everyone. And he said, 'Hey, I know these guys, I am just gonna tell them that everything was cool, that we just wanted to have a good time.'"

"And then what happened?"

"Kevin approached the defendant and started to tell him that everything was cool. The defendant threw a punch at him and knocked him down. I guess Kevin's approach works better with the ladies."

* * *

Assault with Intent to Kill While Armed (*shooting at a basketball court*)

AUSA to witness

"Did anything unusual happen?"

"No."

"Did you hear shots?"

"Yes."

Juror to witness (free-lance photographer who happened to take photos before and after the shooting, but kept his head down behind a basketball pole while the shooting took place)

"So it was almost like the movie *Blow-Up*?"

"Yeah, it was almost like a Pulitzer Prize."

* * *

Armed Robbery

Victim (cab driver)

"He grabbed me from behind and put a knife to my throat. He wanted me to give him my money but he was holding me so tight and with the knife on my throat, I couldn't move."

* * *

Juror (with Eastern European accent) to another juror (African American woman) during break:

"It is strange to think about it, but I grew up on lots of anti-American propaganda. A big chunk of it was about how bad the conditions here in the US were for American blacks. I remember this one book vividly—it was a story of a black soldier returning home in uniform from fighting in World War Two and he is on a bus somewhere in the South, and this elderly black woman is told that she has to yield a seat for a white person, and the soldier tries to defend the lady and is himself forced to leave the bus. The person who orders him off the bus is this repulsive capitalist type with a cigar and a top hat pointing with his thumb over his shoulder. And of course, nobody believed this propaganda about the US, and I remember later on reading about the South before the civil rights era and learning that things were much worse than communist propaganda tried to make us believe."

* * *

Armed Robbery

AUSA to witness (defendant's relative)

"Have you ever seen the defendant with a gun?

"No. Between the two of us, I was the one with a gun."

* * *

Assault with Dangerous Weapon, Assault with Significant Bodily Injury *(workplace altercation)*

AUSA to witness (store manager)

"Where were you when you heard the screams?"

"I was in the toilet."

"What did you do when you heard the screams?"

"I tried to hurry up my number one and went outside."

Victim (being informed about his 6th Amendment right to have the assistance of a lawyer in Grand Jury proceedings)

"Yeah, I want a lawyer because I don't know what happened. I asked for a screwdriver and the fellow hit me on the head with a hammer."

* * *

Assault with Dangerous Weapon

AUSA introduction

"The incident took place in a neighborhood frequented by transgender prostitutes. The victims, who came from Maryland, and were visiting the place for the first time were hanging out—drinking, smoking, and flirting with passers-by. It isn't clear if they had realized the nature of the neighborhood. At one point, two of them decided to visit the local CVS to buy cigarettes, where they exchanged words with an individual who got offended by the way they addressed him. A policeman who happened to be at the CVS intervened and ordered the individual to leave, which he did. Nobody realized at the time that the individual was an intoxicated, off-duty police officer who subsequently assaulted the victims with his service weapon."

* * *

AUSA to witness (victim, age 18)

"What were you doing at that location?"
"Hanging out."
"Inside the car or outside?"
"Both."
"Were you doing anything in particular?"
"Smoking tree."
"Tree?"
"Weed."
AUSA to jury: "Marijuana."
Witness to jury: "Cannabis."

* * *

Felon in Possession *(nighttime exchange of gun fire in a parking lot of a housing project.)*

AUSA to witness (age 13)

"Did you see his gun?"
"No."
"How do you know he was shooting?"
"I saw flashes."
"Where did you see the flashes, near his leg or his head?"
"No, near his hand."

* * *

Armed Robbery, Kidnapping, Felon in Possession *(street crime)*

AUSA to witness (victim, high school freshman)

"What did they take from you?"
"My cell phone."
"What else?"
"The charger."
"What else?"

"Five dollars."

"Did they say anything to you?"

"They said that if I run, they would shoot me."

"What happened after they took those things?"

"They made me show them how to change the password. I had to do that for them like 10 times. And then he forgot his password and I had to show him again."

* * *

Juror (retired economist) to other jurors

"The stupidity of some of these crimes is unbelievable. You feel like rather than indicting them, you want to ask the prosecutor to send them a simple message that they are too stupid to make a living from crime. Perhaps all that we are doing here is getting rid of the really stupid ones and improving the average quality of criminals in the city."

* * *

Assault with Dangerous Weapon

AUSA to witness:

"What happened when she came home?"

"She looked at my face and started to cry."

"What was she saying?"

"She said, 'Oh my God. Look at what they did to your face.'"

"Why didn't you tell the police about it?"

"I didn't think they would care."

* * *

Assault with Intent to Kill while Armed *(hoodlums beefing with each other)*

AUSA to witness (teenage girl)

"Do you know of the beef between the neighborhoods?"

"Yes."

"What is your understanding?"

"When they see one of the other people, they shoot."

"What was the victim doing before getting shot?"

"He was running."

"Was he saying anything?"

"He was saying, 'I'm gonna get these niggers.'" *(She slaps her hand on her mouth.)*

"It's okay to curse here."

* * *

Felony Threats *(neighbors' dispute)*

AUSA to witness

"Were they saying anything to you?"

"They were talking about bald-headed bitches."

"What did they mean?"

"We have short hair."

"What did he say in particular?"

"'I'll beat the shit out of both of you bald-headed bitches.'"

* * *

Assault with Intent to Kill While Armed *(prison stabbing)*

Juror to witness (brought from jail in orange suit, handcuffs, and leg irons)

"The security camera doesn't seem to show anything happening in the corridor before the stabbing."

"?"

"Well, *something* must have happened to cause the stabbing."

"?"

"Was there any tension there?"

"I didn't notice nothing."

* * *

Assault with Dangerous Weapon *(knife)*

AUSA's introduction

"This case started with a disputed drug deal. The dispute took place in the defendant's apartment. You will see evidence that the defendant was running a crack house as well as a house of prostitution. His apartment was divided by hanging sheets into small cubicles. On the wall, he had a sign with what was called 'Hospitality Rules.' According to these rules, the spaces rented for up to 30 minutes and the basic rate was $5."

* * *

AUSA to witness (victim)

"How did the dispute start?"

"I agreed to buy some drugs but when I weighed them, it turned out to be short. The defendant kept pressuring me to buy it and I finally agreed. The defendant then said that because I bought these drugs in his apartment, I owed him a share. I became angry that he was trying to cheat me and tried to run out of the apartment. The defendant tried to stop me."

"Did you do anything on the way out?"

"Yes, to even things out, I grabbed the defendant's digital scale and took it with me."

* * *

Possession with Intent to Distribute, Possession of Firearm

AUSA to witness

"How much money did you have on you?"

"Almost four hundred dollars."

"Where did you get this money?"

"I borrowed if from my uncle to unsuspend my driving license."

"Why was your driving license suspended?"

"I owed money for child support."

"How much money did you owe?"

"Almost eleven hundred dollars."

"What is your child support payment?"

"60 dollars a month."

* * *

Theft, Conspiracy to Commit Theft *(stealing books from a university bookstore)*

AUSA to witness (store manager)

"What did you do when you realized that you had an inventory shortfall?

"I reviewed our surveillance tapes."

"Did you see anything?"

"I saw the defendants stealing books."

"How did you know they were stealing books?"

"They were doing the opposite of what I was paying them to do."

"What were you paying them to do?"

"Bringing boxes of books from the loading dock and shelving them."

"And what did the tapes show?"

"They showed the defendants taking books off the shelves, putting them in boxes, and bringing them down to the loading dock."

* * *

Armed Robbery *(of cab drivers)*

AUSA to witness (defendant's mother)

"Where does you son sleep most nights?"

"Either with his baby mother or with his foster mother."

"At what time did he come to your house."

"At 6 AM."

"Do you know why he came to your house so early?"

"Yes."

"Why?"

"His foster mother went to work and he isn't allowed to stay there while she isn't home."

"When he came into the house, where did he go?"

"Into my bedroom."

"Your son sleeps in your bedroom?"

"Yes."

"Where do you sleep?"

"On the couch."

"Why?"

"To watch the door."

* * *

1st Degree Murder *(attempted robbery of drug dealer)*

AUSA to witness (victim's brother and defendant's cousin)

"Have you ever seen the defendant with a gun?"

"He showed me a pistol once."

"Why?"

"He wanted me to go robbing with him."

"What was your response?"

"I told him he would be better off with a revolver."

* * *

Assault with Intent to Kill While Armed *(street shooting)*

AUSA's introduction

"The victim, who was drunk, was standing in front of the club insulting passers-by; in particular, he insulted the defendant's sister by saying to her 'suck my ass, you dick bitch.' She called her brother on her cell phone; he came by car and, from across the street, shot the victim twice."

* * *

AUSA to witness to the shooting

"Are you currently under the influence of any drugs?"

"Yes, I am."

"What drugs?"

"Cocaine, heroin, and PCP."

"You mean you used these drugs today?"

"Yes."

"When exactly did you take these drugs?"

"Well, I smoked the PCP right outside the building."

* * *

Homicide *(family altercation)*

AUSA's introduction

"The defendant was exchanging words with her half-brother. She said to him, 'Stop talking or I will stab you.' The defendant did not stop talking and was stabbed."

* * *

AUSA to witness (age 75, father to both the victim and defendant)

"The defendant, your daughter, how old is she?"

"Eighteen."

"Was she living at your house?"

"She stayed there from time to time."

"What happened on this occasion?"

"She came into the house and went to her room"

"What do you mean, 'her room'?"

"The room where she used to live."

"What happened then?"

"She took the covers off the bed, and the sheets, and took them outside and put them in the trash."

"Why did she do it?"

"I don't know. I just wanted to watch TV."

"Could it be that your daughter was upset that your son's daughter was living in that room?"

"All of it is my son's wife's fault. Wherever she goes, she creates friction. I want to call her names but I stop myself."

* * *

Assault with Dangerous Weapon (*altercation in club*)

AUSA to witness (who suffered serious head injuries [300 stiches and risk of blindness] as a result of having a champagne bottle thrown at her)

"What happened then?"

"A big party came into the small back room."

"Was there anything special about them?"

"They were rowdy and all dressed in white. I think they came from New Jersey."

"Anything else?"

"There was one gentleman who was drinking champagne from a bottle and groping ladies' rear ends."

"What were you doing?"

"I was making sure my back was to the wall."

* * *

AUSA to witness (husband of woman who was groped)

"What was the purpose of your visit to the club?"

"We were celebrating my wife's birthday."

"How did the altercation start?

"I told the gentleman who groped my wife not to do it again."

"The gentleman in a checkered shirt?"

"Yes."

"And then what happened?"

"He seemed to take it on board. However, two of his friends came over and started to threaten to beat the shit out of me for being disrespectful to their friend."

"What did you do?

"I told them it was juvenile."

"What happened then?"

"I saw the gentleman in a checkered shirt climb on a couch with a bottle in his hand. He drank from it and then seemed poised to throw it. I yelled at him not to do it and pushed against people in front of me to get to him. I was grabbed by several men who punched and kicked me. I ended up on the floor with blood on my face. I also realized that I lost a tooth when I was kicked in the face."

"When you got up were there any participants of the fight still around."

"No, the room was almost empty. One man from the party with the guy with the checkered shirt was still around. He was looking at me."

"Did he say anything?"

"Yes."

"What did he say?"

"We left you leaking."

"What did he mean?"

"I think he meant that they left me bleeding."

* * *

Murder (*knife fight between high school kids over supposed theft*)

AUSA to witness (age 14, former girlfriend of the defendant, mother of his four-month-old child)

"When we talked previously, you didn't want to say anything, isn't that right?"

"I did not."

"Why?"

"I knew he was gonna go to jail, but I didn't want my words to do it."

* * *

Felony Murder while Armed (*attack on a cabdriver*)

AUSA to jury

"This incident took place the day before yesterday. Late at night, the defendant wanted to come into the city with his girl-friend. They called a cab. Once the cabdriver was told of their destination, he demanded a down payment of $20 which the defendant paid. When they arrived at their destination, the fare was $27.75. The defendant said he had no more money so his girlfriend paid $5. The cabdriver insisted on being paid the full fare. The defendant found $2. They still owed 75 cents. The girlfriend went to the defendant's aunt's house to ask for the money. The defendant stayed behind. Moments later, the defendant appeared at his aunt's house walking from a different direction. He refused to talk about what had happened with the cabdriver."

* * *

AUSA to witness (defendant's aunt)

"Did you talk to the defendant after he had been arrested?"
"Yes. He called me from prison."
"What did he say?
"He said he didn't do it."
"What did you say?"
"I asked him if he believed in God."
"What did he say?"
"He said yes. I told him to say his prayers."

The Thingly Nature of the Thing

Shya Scanlon

The wind chime on Greg's house next door had the hollow sound of pennies dropping into a jar. Shya was waiting for his friend Mark, and Dora's friend Donna, who'd decided to drive together to Providence from New York City. They'd never met, but both Dora and Shya agreed their friends would enjoy the drive, and one another, so Dora had set it up, even booking the rental car. "Get something sexy," Shya had said—Donna and Mark were both single. Shya sat in an uncomfortable antique rocker locked to the porch with a bike chain, and watched for a canary yellow Mustang while the wind picked up, and the sound, those coins now all but pouring in. It was Friday night. It was getting late. It was summer.

Dora poked her head out of the screen door after she'd put their daughter to bed. "I think Sonora's finally asleep," she said.

"Have you ever noticed that Greg's chime sounds like coins falling into a jar?"

Dora listened.

"Do you think that was intentional?" Greg owned a strip club by the port, and had a side business as an erotic photographer.

"I don't know," Dora said. "It maybe sounds like the first penny in an empty jar, but each time it's the same. Where are the other pennies going?"

Shya stood, hearing a car. "I didn't think of that," he said. "It's Sisyphusian."

The car was a cab.

"Probably not intentional, then."

"You never know." Dora closed the screen door softly. Anything was possible with Greg.

Shya watched Dora through the window as she straightened up the living room in preparation for their guests. He hadn't been feeling close, lately. There'd been no fighting, really, but a distance had grown between them, and worse, they seemed to have eased into it without much struggle. They spoke seldom, meeting at home in between errands and various summer administrative duties for the neighboring universities where they taught. They stood aside to let one another pass. And yet, it wasn't even tense.

The wind abated, the coins slowed, and Shya recalled an episode of *The Twilight Zone* where a man, after asking a genie for infinite wealth, was rewarded with a pocket that contained a penny each time he reached in. He'd seen it as a child, and at the time this cynical trick had contributed to Shya's suspicions about wishing: it just seemed fishy. Right now, Shya wished on the falling phantom pennies that Mark and Donna would get there soon; he'd had a few beers, was tired, and strangely irritated by the thought of having more people in the house, though he'd been looking forward to it for weeks.

His phone rang. It was Mark.

"So," Shya said. "The pennies provide."

"What? We're almost there. We just missed our exit."

There was enough giggling in the background to suggest Shya and Dora had been right about how well their friends would get along. "Have you been drinking?"

"No. Gah! Yes. We stopped at a place called Bugaboo Creek. Buga-*boo*!" More giggling.

"Right, well, drive safe, okay? If you guys get killed it would ruin the whole weekend."

"The GPS says we'll be there in less than three minutes."

"Perfect. We look forward to it."

"Two."

"Mark, Sonora's in bed, okay? So try to keep it down when you get here."

"One and change."

"Mark?"

The line went dead. Shya was going to call back, but heard squealing tires in the distance, a revving engine, and moments later the Mustang turned onto their street and roared toward him. It pulled into his neighbor's driveway, and Mark got out, grinning.

"Yellow?" he said. "Did it have to be yellow?"

Mark was a big man, tall and solid, and as usual he was dressed in delicate clothing, carefully unmatched. He'd let his curly red hair grow long, and it stood up from his head like strong punctuation. Shya went to help with their luggage, and gave Mark a hug. Donna got out, too, and kissed him on the cheek.

"I take it you two are getting along," Shya observed.

"We're getting married," Donna said. "We've already booked tickets to Vegas."

"I'm seriously about to rape this woman," Mark said, pulling bags from the back seat. "I mean, rape in a good way."

Donna ran up the stairs to the porch. "Dora," she called. "Dora?" She was small, slight, similar in build to her best friend, Shya's wife. Her quick brown hair shot out to one side. Shya watched her go, quietly giving up on keeping Sonora in bed.

"Vegas, huh?" he said.

Mark owned his own company—a line of stuffed animals called Oopsies that said cringe-worthy, sexually implicit things like "Stop touching me there!" when squeezed. He had a history of spontaneous romantic expenditure.

"Well," Mark said, "we'll see how the weekend goes."

* * *

Donna stood in the dining room window, sipping at scalding coffee. The night had been a late one, apparently, but not for Shya, who'd had too much too soon, and had snuck off to bed in the middle of a discussion about obscenity in popular culture—"Popular culture *is* obscenity," Donna had shouted not long before he turned in. Donna ran an art gallery in Chelsea, so she would know, but Shya hadn't felt that it was a very helpful definition.

"Your neighbor is waving at me," she now said dully. "Who waves at people through the window?"

"He probably wants you to pose for him," Dora said, entering from the kitchen with a banana. She was on the "banana diet," which meant, as far as Shya could tell, exactly what it seemed to, only less.

"Oh, *he's* the photo guy? Maybe I should give Mark a couple of pictures to remember me by."

Mark was still asleep, though Donna had already indicated that union had been achieved in the guest room last night.

"He wanted to do me—ha!—to photograph me, I mean, when I was pregnant," Dora said. "In the nude, of course."

"Yuck," said Donna.

"That's what I thought. But now I'm sorry I didn't."

They had a rough outline for their day: a scenic drive to Newport—"With the top down," Mark had made clear—and then a backyard BBQ. But they felt flexible. Both Shya and Dora had already finished tweaking their syllabi for next year and taken the kid to her best friend's house, the dog was at the hospital—they were free. Free for hours and hours. Dora came up behind Shya and, as if sensing his thoughts, said she hoped Brenda Sue was alright.

"I bet she's lonely," she said.

"I bet she's on drugs," said Shya.

"What's the deal with your dog, again?" Mark shuffled out of the guestroom and sat down at the dining table, rubbing his eyes.

"This man did truly tasteless things to me last night," said Donna, frowning at Shya's friend and retreating down the hallway to the kitchen.

Mark rolled his eyes. "You've got interesting friends," he said to Donna, who nodded.

"She has stomach cancer," Donna said.

Mark's hands fell to the table and he sat upright in his chair, then leaned forward and in a half-whisper, said, "She has *cancer?*"

"The dog, dumbass," Shya said. "Brenda Sue."

"It's her second surgery. We get her back on Monday."

"God," Shya said, "don't remind me."

Dora shoved him and stuck out her tongue. "Shya's not looking forward—*no one* is looking forward, but especially Shya—to the kind of care Brenda is going to need when she gets home."

"We're going to have to hold her while she relieves herself," Shya said.

Mark stood up, shaking his head and waving his hands in the air. "Oh god," he said, "seriously. Too early for this. That's horrible and I love you but really, please." He went to the kitchen, leaving Shya and Dora alone at the table.

Shya reached across for Dora's hands, and she put down her coffee to hold them, looking into his eyes. He suddenly remembered her coming to bed last night and trying to rouse him, reaching her hand into his underwear and tugging drunkenly at his soft, sleeping penis. He'd wanted to match her enthusiasm, and in his groggy state he'd fumbled around with her shirt, but in the end it had seemed unrealistic, and they'd both chuckled ruefully before passing out in one another's arms. They should have known better. Shya gave her hands a brief squeeze and let go, standing.

"She's going to be okay," he said. "Should we do food?"

"Food," she said. "Foooooood."

* * *

It was an oozing, ripe summer day, and as they cruised east through all the perfect New England towns sprinkled along Route 114, the convertible filled with the smell of cut grass and salt air. Shya drove, Dora smoked—something she only did when Donna was in town—and the lovebirds laughed and cuddled and playfully slapped in the backseat, seemingly overcome. It was truly stunning, and Shya felt stunned. He stole glances in the rearview mirror, but also at Dora, to see how much attention she was paying their friends. Their antics seemed to amplify the calm routine of his relationship into a kind of embarrassing solemnity. The truth was, his feelings for Dora hadn't disappeared. They were there, only muffled. He could feel them beneath some new layer of ... of what, he couldn't quite say. They hadn't had sex in months.

Shya was looking at Mark whisper something into Donna's ear when her eyes bulged and she pushed him out of the way. "Holy shit," she said. "Pull over!"

Shya braked too quickly and the heavy yellow car skidded a bit before easing off the road. He looked back to see how close they'd come to being rear-ended, but the white Suburban behind them only slowed down as it passed, revealing an old woman drinking something through a straw.

"Change of plans," Donna said. "We *must* go see that windmill."

She pointed toward the water, and sure enough, an enormous, lone windmill spun well above the tops of full grown oaks, its long white blades lumbering through the air in slow motion.

Dora turned around. "Are you fucking kidding me? You almost got us killed!"

"You're getting soft, honey," said Donna. She looked at Shya. "What say? Windmill? Or no windmill."

Shya found a road that seemed like it would get them close, and parked at the foot of a long dirt drive with a chain across it. They started walking.

"So, good news, did I tell you?" Mark said. "I got a call from Ben Stiller's production company. They want to use something from the new line in some *Meet the Parents*-type movie they're making."

"That's great!" Shya said. "Though *Meet the Parents* was horrible." Mark had always been one of the few people in Shya's life whose success didn't feel threatening. It was either because they'd been friends for so long, or because his medium, such as it was, was so obviously populist—something you either *did* or *didn't* do. Shya decidedly *didn't*, and that was fine. His work would never appear in a Ben Stiller film.

"Ben Stiller is a god," Donna said.

"*Zoolander* is one of my all-time favorite movies," agreed Dora.

Shya turned to Dora, surprised. "Really?"

Dora shrugged.

Donna pulled a plastic bag out of her purse, and said, "Let's blaze."

According to a plaque screwed to its base, the windmill was operated by a boarding school called Portsmouth Abbey. On their backs, it towered above them, a luminous, humming thing, both terrible and intensely satisfying. They were stoned.

"I can't believe you smoke pot," Mark said to Donna. He'd smoked some too, but he was generally, Shya knew, skeptical of illegal drug use.

"Get to know me," she said.

Dora laughed. "Christ," she said. "I miss you, dear."

"Well if you'd ever move back to the city," she said, then scowled at Shya, "*like you plan to...* You'd see me all the time." She sat up. "They said 'One more year' for three years before I stopped listening."

"I remember," Mark said. "Bastards."

They were silent for a while, and Shya remembered having real intentions to return. He remembered, most of all, the ambition that drove those intentions, the raw, certain feeling that New York was "where things happened."

The field in which they lay was littered with small white butterflies that kept flying into their faces. Of course, there were many factors that had kept them from moving, but none were truly prohibitive. They were excuses, not reasons.

"Are these moths," Dora said, "or butterflies?"

Donna flipped her hands in the air, dismissing the question. "All I know is they're not rats."

"For one," Shya said, "Dora and I have great jobs here."

"I hope I never have a job again," Mark said. "I mean, a job job."

Dora rolled onto her side, away from Shya. "I still have contacts in publishing," she said. "I bet I could find something."

"Well," Shya said, irritated—why was she encouraging Donna? "And then there's Sonora. The school system is great out here."

Donna offered Dora a cigarette, and lit one for herself. "I'm always jealous of people who actually grew up in the city," she said. "You don't run into them very much anymore. One of the kids we're showing at the gallery is born and bred, and he's just got this *vitality*. He's got this energy all boxed in under his lonely, tough guy Brando façade. Like he's ready to explode. It's quite thrilling. We've already sold most of his work, and the show isn't until next month."

"What do you think, Dora. Sonora as lonely tough guy?"

Dora laughed. Their daughter was open and joyful, the most magical thing they'd ever seen. They often spoke about her in hushed tones, as if, even in her absence, she'd somehow know how worshipful they were of her, and exploit it. "We don't want her to get a big head," they'd whisper. And then, "Did you hear what she said? 'Birds don't fly, people just sit.' Isn't that amazing? She's brilliant! People sit!" Shya just couldn't imagine her walking down the dark, steel ravines of New York City, a world of banking above her head.

"What are you working on?" Donna asked. "Do we get a peek?"

Shya knew this was coming, and he'd been hoping to avoid the subject. He stood. The windmill was on a small rise, and from it he could see the bay, and beyond that the sea. He faced the wind and closed his eyes, imagining that he too was able to generate the kind of energy being captured behind him. Being created.

"I don't know, maybe. You probably won't like it."

"Shya hasn't even let me see it," Dora said.

"He's probably working with your neighbor," Mark said. "He's doing x-rated oils."

"Now *that* would sell," Donna said.

Shya looked back to see Donna rolling over toward Mark. She reached out and grabbed his jaw, pulled his face toward hers, and kissed him on the mouth. Dora was watching too, and they stopped at the same time, meeting one another's eyes and quickly looking away. Was she embarrassed that they weren't kissing too? Shya felt inclined to go lie down with her, but thought it might seem too forced, too deliberately competitive.

Shya and Dora were married. They had nothing to prove by aping a love-struck, weekend fling.

"So," Shya asked, "what does the Oopsie in Stiller's film say?"

Mark pushed Donna away in mock disgust and brushed some grass off his shirt, his big, red afro wobbling in the wind.

"Does this mean you love me?"

* * *

They picked up Sonora on the way home, who, once she'd seen the Mustang, ran out of the house without saying goodbye to her friend, Nadia, or to Nadia's mother, who looked at Shya judgmentally, his daughter's rudeness clearly evidence of poor parenting.

"Yellow is her favorite color," Shya said apologetically.

Nadia's house was set far back from the street as if trying to retreat from public view. He and Dora felt, actually, that Nadia was a little too oblivious for Sonora, too soft-minded. But their daughter was always excited to visit them, and Dora suspected it was because they got to watch TV and eat junk food.

When he got back to the car, Sonora was in the backseat, where there seemed to be some kind of problem with the seatbelt situation.

"I'll give her mine," Mark said. "I wasn't using it anyway. You didn't hear that, Sonora."

"But then you'll basically be sharing Donna's seat," Dora said. "It seems dumb to have all that weight loose back there."

"No offense taken, Dora," Mark said.

Shya got in, glad he was driving.

"Sonora, honey, you're going to sit up front with mommy, okay? We'll share the seatbelt."

"Yay!" Sonora shouted, and scrambled over the emergency brake onto her mother's lap.

"It's illegal, you know," Shya said. "We'll get pulled over if they catch us."

"So avoid the police," Dora said.

They pulled out of the driveway, and Shya hoped Nadia's mother wasn't watching. They weren't very far away from their house, but because of all the one-way streets, avoiding arterials meant they had to go out of their way. Dora asked Sonora about what she'd been doing all day, but Sonora wasn't very responsive, intent on making the most of her ride.

"You didn't happen to choose this car because of you know who," Shya said, nodding at their daughter.

Dora shrugged, admitting defeat.

"Wow," Shya said. "That's sexy."

Why had she been sabotaging him all day? He tried to glare at her until she noticed, but he was forced to pay attention to the road, and upon arrival they all peeled off to separate corners of the house. Donna and Mark curled into the guestroom for a nap, Dora took Sonora to the backyard to help clean up for the BBQ, and Shya retreated to his office, where he drew the shades, locked the door, and pulled down his pants.

Masturbation had been serving many functions for Shya, recently. There was the traditional relief of stress, there was comfort and of course simple perversion, but there had also arrived a more sinister purpose. Shya had taken to masturbating for revenge. It was an act, on these occasions, against his wife, against their marriage, against the possibility of arousal. He turned off the sound on the PC and went to a bookmark folder called Research. He scrolled down the list, past Teen-Fuck, past SaphicLove and FuckTube, past AnalVirgin and past VIPTwins, then changed his mind and clicked on VIPTwins. He didn't have subscriptions to any of these sites; he was content to go through their "Guided Tours" and watch the sample clips, plenty long enough, he found—even at one or two minutes—for his purposes.

The house was quiet, which was unusual, and once Shya began to warm himself up, he found that in this silence even the small noises of his hand hitting the base of his penis was audible, even distinguishable, so he had to be careful. His wife and daughter were having some kind of argument in the back-yard, and he tried to block them out, fill his head instead with these two thin, gaunt girls with straight blond hair. They looked young, and indeed one of them had braces. Their small breasts rose from their supine bodies like peaks of meringue as they lay back on a large, sheetless bed letting two bald men eat them out. In the pictures of them kissing, their differences stood out—one had more freckles, while the other's cheeks looked almost sallow—but from behind they looked identical, their bony asses raised and spread to reveal the identical pink flesh of their shaved vulvas and clean, puckered sphincters. They ran their lips up and down the shaft of one man's penis, staring one another in the eyes. It was not erotic in the least, but for Shya this wasn't the point, and it wasn't long before he ejaculated. He came in his hand, which he then wiped with a Kleenex. His body felt slack and his testicles tingled. There would be no way, he thought with satisfaction and self-loathing, that he'd be able to get it up later that night, should Dora come on to him again.

* * *

"I'm sure," Dora said, "that yes, it's about puzzle solving." Dinner had been eaten, and they were in the back yard, drinking wine, digesting, and talking about what it was that drew Dora's students to geology. "But it's not irrelevant like puzzles always are. Soulless. If they wanted soulless puzzles they could go into math."

"I think I actively resist being a part of something larger," said Donna.

"You mean the art world?" Mark said, and poured himself more wine.

"You look at a piece of art," she continued, "as something in and of itself. Something entire. Yes, fine, there are schools and trends and whatever but that's all academic bullshit. No offense, Shya. The artist and his work are ultimately alone, just like the art and the viewer are alone once it's done. It's the beginning and the end. I admire that. All your effort piecing things together would drive me crazy. Especially things you can't even see!"

Dora shrugged slightly and hugged Sonora, who was sitting on her lap.

"I don't really consider myself an academic," Shya said.

"Pratt just announced a concentration in toy design," Mark said. "Which is really smart, I think. The 'toy' needs to be socially reformulated from an ontological perspective. It's not just a thing to play with—it's a projection of the very nature of play itself."

"Oh please," Donna said. "*Your* toy is a projection."

"What do you think," Dora said to Sonora, who was yawning. "Do you think the significance of toys is underestimated?"

"The significance of play!" Mark said, loudly, a bit drunk.

They all looked at the girl, and she buried her head into Dora's chest.

"It's okay, sweetheart," Shya said. "Uncle Mark is overcompensating."

It was late evening, and the trees in the yard swayed darkly against a clear sky drained of nearly all color but still lit, a pale, gray sky, a frail sky. This was high summer, perfect summer. The humidity had been swept from the air by a breeze too light to feel, the temperature making their skin disappear. Shya breathed deeply, wanting an imprint of that moment, wanting it inside him.

Then Greg called over from his backyard.

"Nice night," he said. Greg had a voice just gravelly enough to make even the simplest statement sound vaguely grotesque. They all turned to find him leaning against the white picket fence, his bald head fairly glowing, his white shirt open to his sternum.

"So you're the pornographer," said Donna.

"Jesus," Dora said. "Sorry Greg. Donna is from New York, where they don't have manners."

Greg laughed. "No worries. Pleased to meet you, Donna. I like a woman who speaks her mind."

"A *woman*," Donna said.

"But if I may clarify, however, I take erotic photographs. I don't do porn."

"That's what I told them," Shya said. "There's a difference."

"Porn is you take something erotic and take out the art."

Donna stood up and began walking toward the fence. Shya half-expected her to get into an argument, even slap the man, but instead she asked for his card. "I want to see for myself," she said.

"The website is right on there," he said. "I think you'll see that I leave the art in."

Donna shook his hand, and it looked to Shya like she was being flirtatious, but it could have just been her way. Greg bid them goodnight and continued on—he was headed to work, he said, at the club.

After he left they all seemed to relax, as though they'd been sucking in their stomachs, puffing out their chests. Shya was embarrassed, a little, at the tacit but obvious fact that they'd all been judging their neighbor. Donna perhaps even openly ridiculing him. It had derailed them, and they gave the evening a silent moment to regain momentum.

"I leave the art in," said Mark, finally. "That's fucking brilliant. F'ing, I mean."

"What's 'leaving the art in,' Mommy?" said Sonora.

The question was so strange that they all laughed. There was something obvious about it, something crude.

"It's what daddy does," she said. "He leaves the art in."

"Ha! I'm not sure how much art I'm leaving in."

There was a long pause, then Dora stood.

"Great idea, Sonora," she said. "Let's go look at Daddy's work."

She held out her hand and, when Sonora grabbed it, started walking toward the shed. Shya watched them walk inside, then looked at Donna and Mark, who were waiting for his move. "Shit," he said. "Okay."

Donna stood and clapped her hands in a girlish burst, then pulled Mark across the yard. Shya followed them, looking around at the empty bottles and paper plates he passed on his way. It felt strange to leave such things around, strange not to have Brenda Sue to worry about. It was the first time he'd missed her since they'd dropped her off for the procedure. How odd to miss having to go out of one's way, he thought. To miss being bothered.

When he entered, they were standing before a painting he'd been struggling with for weeks. They were silent, looking back and forth between the five foot canvas fixed to the wall and the small subject, propped up on an old wooden chair.

"You're painting ... a painting?" Mark said as Shya came to stand beside them.

"It's a print," said Donna. "And it's perfectly legitimate."

The subject was indeed a print: a fish print he'd made years ago, the year before Sonora was born, with a rainbow trout he'd caught on a trip with Dora's brother Doug.

"Remember that fish?" Shya asked.

"Oh god," Dora said. It was an unpleasant memory from an unpleasant time. "He wouldn't eat the damn thing!"

It had become symbolic, at the time, of Shya's ambivalence about a great many things, and by the time he'd decided to prepare it, the trout was in no condition to be eaten. He'd brought it to his studio and let it rot, then did several prints of it—a testament to the impact of his inaction. A reminder.

"Why wouldn't you eat the fish, Daddy?"

"I guess I wasn't hungry."

Donna stepped forward to examine the large oil: an attempt to recreate that fish. It was photorealistic in detail, its original colors—gone from the fish in the print, for which he'd used grays and dull reds to reflect decay—were restored, the blues and iridescent greens, hints of purples and pinks, all there across the man-size surface.

"You'd have to show the print along with it, of course," Donna said.

"Show? I doubt I'll be showing anything."

"Are there more?"

Shya looked at Donna, trying to determine her level of sincerity. Did she actually think there was something here? She hadn't liked his work in years.

"There are a few more, yes."

In fact, there were over a dozen more, all large oils of small still-lifes and prints he'd done before Sonora was born, each one an idealized version of the decrepit, rotting, or otherwise flawed original subject. A turned leaf green again. A broken rake whole. Shya had been working on something he felt was possibly clinically indulgent, and had been afraid to show them even, as Dora had said, to his wife, to his family. He'd been ashamed of them. He looked at Dora now, who was smiling.

"I understand this," she said softly.

She slowly moved to him and put her arm around his waist and together they looked back at the fish, the big beautiful fish.

"Well, I wouldn't say I 'understand' it," said Mark, "but I'm thinking about you out here painting your fish, all alone, and it kind of breaks my heart." He came to Shya's other side and put his arm around Shya's shoulder. "In a good way, I mean."

"See," Shya said, "this is kind of why I didn't want anyone to see these. There's basically nothing worse than having someone look at your work and feel sorry for you."

"I don't feel sorry for you," said Donna. "I feel excited for you. You need to show this. There is real neurosis here. And it's refreshingly free of ... of obscenity! Weren't we just talking about that? I mean, look at it. Sure, Shakespeare used fish to symbolize sex, but I'm not getting any of that here."

They all nodded, considering the work in this light.

Then Sonora asked, "What's anosis?"

"Neurosis," Donna said. "It's one of the most important ingredients of good art."

"Donna, really," said Dora. "You'll turn our daughter into a monster."

"Rawr!" Sonora threw her hands above her head and began teetering around like Frankenstein.

"See?" said Donna. "Perhaps it's what she wants."

"It's what everybody wants," said Mark.

"Does this mean you love me?"

* * *

Shya woke Sunday to a note explaining that Dora and Donna had left to run an errand. "It's a surprise," it said. It also asked him to clean the kitchen and look after the kid. He followed a bright, chirping laugh into the living room, where Sonora was watching Sunday morning cartoons and eating an English muffin with apricot preserves—something she ate to feel like a grown-up. She looked up at him defensively, and held the remote to her chest.

"Mommy said I could," she said.

"Did your mom say where she was going?"

Sonora shook her head.

"I feel like shit!" Mark called from the guest room.

"See, Sonora? That's what happens when you swear."

He went to the kitchen and began to clean, expecting Mark to help, but after loading the dishwasher he returned to the living room to find him sitting with Sonora, watching cartoons.

"This is amazing," he said.

Shya joined them on the couch.

The show seemed to be about an animate piece of driftwood and the pincers of a lobster that detached, then grabbed onto the driftwood to get washed up on shore, where the pair's misadventures led to a lesson about environmentalism.

"Remember that," Mark said as the show ended, "next time you find a condom on the beach."

Shya stood up. "I don't understand why they have to be so *weird*. Talking animals I get. But a piece of wood? A *part* of an animal? There's a difference between a preschool child and a stoner."

"Right," said Mark. "Preschoolers watch cartoons, stoners make them. I think you have to watch it with an open mind. I mean, ignore the context. Just let the images kind of flow into your head."

Shya looked at Mark to see if he was kidding. He wasn't. "Flow into my head," he repeated.

"Yeah, you know, not uncritically, but—"

"Maybe I'm an academic after all, but in my mind, 'flow' and 'critical' are mutually exclusive."

"Please," Sonora said, taking a bite of her English muffin, "take your conversation to another room please."

They went into the kitchen, finished cleaning up, then made for the back yard. It was already warm, and lawnmowers had begun to invade the peaceful morning air. Mark had gotten a beer out of the fridge, and he cracked it open, then thoughtfully turned the can in his hand before taking a sip. As long as Shya had known Mark, he'd always been fascinated by what Heidegger had called the *thingly nature of the thing*.

"Let me guess," Shya said. "It puts the can in the age of mechanical reproduction."

Mark peered at Shya over the top of his beer. "Asshole," he belched. "Besides, there's no can in mechanical."

"Well, it's always like you're seeing everything for the first time."

"Are you kidding? I've seen this can a million times. Because I'm an alcoholic. Seriously, though, this can is the same or almost the same as just about every can I've ever seen. The trick is," he said, "to recognize the sameness and…"

"And what?"

"Celebrate it."

Shya laughed, and went inside to get a beer.

"I'm sorry. Are we on *Oprah*?"

He peeked in on his daughter, and watched silently for a moment as she giggled over the antics of a purple bottle cap with three legs, one of which was rebelling. The bottle cap walked awkwardly across a bright white table, falling over forks and a piece of bowtie pasta.

"Pasta mañana," it said.

Sonora laughed, though Shya was almost certain she didn't speak a word of Spanish. He looked at her, his daughter. It was beyond him, all this, but not unhappily so, and he felt somehow content in his befuddlement. He returned to the backyard, where Mark was typing something into his phone.

"Texting Donna?"

"What? No, I just had an idea for a new Oopsie."

"Let me hear it."

"Okay, but only if we can watch cartoons afterward."

"You want to watch more cartoons?"

"That's the line."

Shya let this sink in. "That's sick," he said.

"It is what you bring to it."

"Bullshit."

Mark finished his beer. "Okay, okay," he said, shaking his head. "You're right. Sometimes you just begin to see things as formal exercises. I work within these constraints, you know, and …"

"You have to pull back once in a while, I mean come on."

A dog started barking, then someone shouted "no" and it stopped. Mark inhaled deeply, sampling the summer air.

"Something strange happened to me this morning," he said.

Shya took a big swallow of beer. It was cheap beer, Rainier—the kind Mark swore by—and it went down smoothly, like spit.

"Donna threw up on my dick," Mark said.

"Are you really telling me this?"

"Wouldn't you want to know? She threw up on my dick. Has that ever happened to you?"

"I've never thrown up on someone's dick, no."

"It was a rise-and-shiner, and she was really going to town. I'd kind of lain back on the bed and wasn't watching anymore, trying to hold it in, you know? And then I felt this warmness all over my belly and legs, and my first thought was 'Holy shit, I pissed on her face.' She didn't make any puking sounds or anything. I look down, and she's looking at me, just scared as hell, her eyes huge."

"What did you do?"

"I started to laugh."

"No shit."

"We both laughed for like ten minutes. What else could we do?"

"This is in the spare room?" Shya said. He immediately started thinking about whether he'd have to throw the futon out.

"Don't worry—we cleaned it up. It didn't really get on the bed."

They sat there in silence for a minute, and Shya was trying to decide if he should have another beer.

"I guess what I'm trying to say is—"

"You're *trying to say* something with that?"

"What I'm trying to say is," and here Mark began to laugh, "someone could be throwing up on your dick."

Shya stared hard at his friend. This was someone who, nearly forty, was living a life almost identical to the one he was living years ago after they'd left Seattle, ready to take over New York. Mark had come much closer to achieving that vague goal, of course. He was still there, for one. Mark got up and went inside, for more beer no doubt, leaving Shya alone with the growing grass, the sighing leaves. The lawnmower had stopped, he noticed. Birds chirped. Shya closed his eyes. For a moment, he felt entirely at peace.

"Yoo-hoo! Shya!"

He opened his eyes to see Donna, then Dora, emerge from the back door of Greg's house. They were giggling and smoking, wearing heavy red lipstick and mascara. They were drunk. Greg poked his head out the door behind them, and watched them walk to the front of the house, then looked over at Shya and shook his head.

"You got two wild, gorgeous ladies there," he said. He whistled and then shut the door.

Shya watched a passing jet paint its contrails on the sky, and listened to the wild "ladies" make their rowdy way through the house, picking up Sonora in the front room, then Mark in the kitchen, and within moments they were all outside, laughing and dancing on the lawn. Mark handed Shya a beer.

"You boys are in for a treat," Donna slurred.

"What treat?" Sonora asked. "Can I have a treat?"

Dora wagged her finger. "It's not for you, missy," she said. Then when she saw Sonora's face change to register complaint, she softened. "Don't worry, dear. You'll get a treat."

Sonora whooped with joy, and flailed around with Donna and Mark, who were doing a makeshift Macarena.

"So when do we get to see the pictures?" Shya said.

"He said they'd be ready in a week," Dora said, wrapping her arms around him.

"Did you do any together?" Mark asked.

"Maybe we did," Donna said, "and maybe we didn't."

Mark embraced her in a slow dance, and the two of them spun slowly around as Shya watched. When Donna's back was turned, Mark's face appeared over her shoulder and he brought his finger up to his mouth, pointed down his throat, and stuck out his tongue.

* * *

That night they'd ordered pizza, not wanting to prepare, to cook, to clean, and after dinner—after Sonora had been put to bed—they'd sat around the table, opening wine and beginning their protracted goodbyes. It was their last night together, and already Donna and Dora were talking about when they'd see one another next. Dora made it to the city two or three times a year, but because of school, her daughter, and now of course her dog, she couldn't make definitive plans.

"Remember when you worked for *Elle*?" Donna asked wistfully. "You were always traveling. You loved it."

"It wore me out," corrected Dora.

"I read about this guy," Mark said, "the heir to some Greek shipping company, who's been basically living in an airplane. But not on his own plane, even though he's probably got like four. He's been flying first class around the world in those private cabins they have on Singapore Air and Qantas and whatever. Just getting in one and setting up shop, taking it back and forth until it's put in the hanger for the annual diagnostic."

Donna screwed her face up as he was talking, and began to shake her head. "What is it with you," she said. "Why all the anecdotes. I've never met someone who's so full of useless anecdotes."

Mark shrugged, and poured himself more wine. "Just trying to keep the conversation from getting too nostalgic."

"Nostalgia," Donna said, "is a perfectly reasonable thing to indulge in among friends. It's what you get for living forty years, and it's nothing to be ashamed of. Maybe if you didn't spend all your time glorifying juvenilia you wouldn't be so uncomfortable with it."

"I thought you didn't like to be part of something larger."

"That's out of context," Donna said.

Shya met Dora's eyes, which shone with something like enjoyment. It felt good to witness something so flagrantly petty, to be outside themselves.

"I'm so glad you two finally met," Dora said.

Shya almost said something about Vegas, but bit his tongue.

Donna changed the subject. "I'm not going to let you off the hook about those oils," she said. "It's not the kind of thing I do at my gallery, but I have connections. Get some fucking slides done and—Jesus I almost said courier. *Mail* them to me. Don't people still mail things?"

"Don't do it," Mark said, "unless we actually get those pictures Greg took."

"Porn for painting," said Donna, slapping her hand on the table. "Fair trade."

"It's not porn," said Dora. "He left the art in."

"Well," said Mark, "hopefully he took out *some* of the art."

Shya shook his head, smiling, not sure he wanted to show the work, not sure he wanted to see the pictures. It was late, and talk died down in deference. Soon they made their way to their respective bedrooms, promising to wake up early enough for breakfast before they left.

It was a close, windless night. Dora did a sweep through the house to make sure the doors were locked, then came to the bedroom, where Shya was trying to read. He was a little drunk, still, and was having a difficult time tracking; he'd been on the same sentence for more than a minute. From the guestroom, Mark and Donna could be heard quarrelling, which they'd been doing on and off all day.

"This is ridiculous," he said, and put the magazine down, giving up.

"I know. What could those two possibly have to fight about already? It's like they're living out a full relationship cycle in the span of three days."

"They're New Yorkers, after all."

Dora sighed, getting into bed.

"You know, Dora, if you want to move back to New York, we'll make it happen."

Dora smiled, nudging him with her shoulder. "It's not that. I was just thinking: we get Brenda Sue back tomorrow."

"And all that goes along with it."

"All that goes along with it, yes. I really missed her over the last few days. Did you miss her?"

Shya looked at his wife. His beautiful wife. He hadn't thought about Brenda Sue once the whole weekend. Had he? He tried to remember. No, he thought.

"Yes," he said.

"Me too," she said, and snuggled up to him.

In the other room, Donna said something loud and they heard a thump. Shya laughed, and so did Dora. They laughed, thinking of their two good friends getting upset over nothing, thinking of how much they'd had to drink that weekend and of the pictures Greg had taken. Shya smoothed Dora's hair down and kissed her head, then she leapt out of bed and went to the oscillating fan by the window. She turned it up, turned it on high, and flooded the dark room with white noise, light wind.

What Wants to Be Shot

Madeline ffitch

E ven now, no one knows what it was like for Thomas J. Jefferson and Flip. J. Jones to be best friends. No one knows
what it was like for them that summer, though each day, Hayworth watched their long involved preference for each other.
They tried to attract the attention of the songbirds in the ash
trees, and they used outdated slurs such as "bulldagger." They
used outdated slurs when they stubbed their toes, or when they
couldn't get the attention of the songbirds in the ash trees. They
hadn't killed anything. They wore matching red trunks, and
nothing else. They had turned brown all over their bodies (this
was from never going inside) and their legs were impossibly
long. Hayworth was Thomas J. Jefferson's girl-cousin, five years
younger, and she loved those two young men as if she herself
wasn't even real.

They all three of them believed in feats of strength, and so
they left the city, and for two days they walked through the long
low spindly woods. First, they came through rows of thin white
tree trunks, and then they came through leaves like light coins,
and finally they came to a four way intersection, arid and still.
Here, there were four empty storefronts facing each other, and
nothing going on, not even a cat going on, only some raccoons
back in the alley, raccoons with dexterous black gloves, like they

all have. Each storefront had a stoop, and each stoop was baked hot in the afternoon sun the day they came to the intersection. They all noticed how quiet it was, as quiet as if they'd drawn the place with a crayon as they came along. So they decided to stay there all summer, and the summer was hot. Thomas J. Jefferson and Flip J. Jones had a pair of .22 rifles between them.

"What are we going to shoot with those rifles?" asked Hayworth. She had looped embroidery floss through the holes in her ears, three strands, orange, mandarin orange, and blood orange. Hayworth had occasionally asked for privacy, but when she got it, it was only a coincidence.

"We'll shoot bottles, and we'll throw my old boots up across the telephone wire, and we'll shoot at them, and we'll shoot anything that bothers us," said Thomas J.

"We don't want a thing to bother us," said Flip J. "You can share my ammunition box, Hayworth."

"You'd better not shoot any of that raccoon family," said Hayworth.

"We'll shoot anything that bothers us," repeated Flip J. He was kind, and he showed his large teeth like blocks of ice, and Hayworth loved him.

Hayworth stepped up onto the stoop behind her so that she was eye level with Flip J. Behind her, the Green River Soda marquee was empty, and the screen door hung open, and they didn't know what could be inside.

"It'll stay much quieter here if you don't go galloping around shooting those raccoons for no reason," said Hayworth.

"See, this is what I mean, goddammit, Hayworth," said Thomas J. "We let you come through the woods with us, we let you drink rum and water with us, and by the way, you've given me no reason to regret that. I like having you here, and Flip J. likes having you here."

"I like you a lot, Hayworth," said Flip J.

"But goddammit," said Thomas J, "if you don't sometimes act just like a seventeen-year-old girl."

"Thomas J, all I'm saying is that we could stay here the whole summer, and there would never be any need to shoot a raccoon," said Hayworth.

"Is that a rule you're making?" asked Thomas J. He cut his eyes down away from her. He practiced proper gun safety.

"I'm not afraid to make it a rule, if you want it like that," said Hayworth.

"What's the rule?" asked Flip J.

No one knows what it's like for two boys to be best friends, but we know a few things, gleaned over the years. We know, for example, that when Flip J. Jones and Thomas J. Jefferson were teenagers, they rode out together one night on a pair of junked bikes, through the city that they came from. Thomas J. pulled ahead, and Flip J. fell behind, though he pushed hard to keep up. We know that Flip J's wheel skidded out. He went over the handlebars, and crunched his head right against the asphalt. It slid, it shaved like a bar of soap. Thomas J. circled back, and when he lifted Flip J. it was bad, it was a stranger he found. Thomas J. taught Flip J. to walk again, and Flip J. learned it good-naturedly and well. Flip J. was rangey and true, and if he didn't like you, you knew it was no use thinking you were any good. Hayworth wanted Flip J. to touch her, and he had never touched her. Yet her cousin, Thomas J. had never protected her from anything.

"The rule is that you can shoot what wants to be shot," said Hayworth.

* * *

Thomas J. knelt, took aim at the storefront window across the street, and crack, and the window was a spider's web. Flip J. said, "'Atta kid," and meant no harm.

"What about that?" Thomas J. asked.

"That window wanted to be shot," said Hayworth.

"'Atta kid," Flip J. said again. Hayworth took her turn next. What wanted to be shot was a dented folding chair set up at the end of the block. She handed the rifle to Flip J. What wanted to be shot was the upstairs window of the empty five and dime. What wanted to be shot were the red roof tiles above the Green River Soda marquee, the rubble of the ex-sidewalk, the beer cans stabbed onto the chain link fence, the lid of each trash can, an unplugged ice machine, and the knothole of the ash tree that stood on the southwest corner all alone.

At dusk, they had gone through Flip J's box of ammunition, and they sat down together to take a rest, Flip J. and Thomas J. on the top step, Hayworth hanging around on the railing. Thomas J. and Flip J. only approved of the liquor that, like burnt sugar, lashed you and was good to take with water. They had some of it now, and they shared it with Hayworth.

"Hayworth would like to marry you someday, Flip J," said Thomas J. Flip J. grinned in his sheepish way. He took a grey dove's feather from the bottom step and twirled it between his fingers.

"But I'm too old for her," said Flip J.

"She doesn't care about that," said Thomas J. "You'd better look out."

"Is that true, Hayworth, what your cousin's always saying?" asked Flip J, keeping his eyes on the feather.

"Maybe it is. There wouldn't be any shame in it," said Hayworth. One of the raccoon family, now that the noise and smoke was over, trotted out into the dim intersection. The three of them watched it. Its back was a steep round hump, small and industrious, the moon stood in the sky, and Thomas J. and Flip J. rose at the same time, and crack, crack, and the raccoon flipped over with no noise, and was still. Dark liquid splashed briefly from it, and went to mud in the dust.

"I told you not to do it, I told you not to!" said Hayworth.

"You told me what, you stupid kid thought you could make up rules at me out here?" asked Thomas J.

"I asked you not to, that's all," said Hayworth.

"You're lucky you're even here," said Thomas J.

"What about you, Flip J? You know that raccoon didn't want to get shot," Hayworth turned to him.

"It's no big deal, Hayworth," said Flip J, smiling and looking at the ground.

"Now what are you going to do?" asked Hayworth.

"What do you mean?" asked Thomas J.

"What are you going to do with it?" asked Hayworth.

"We'll leave it there as a warning to other raccoons," said Thomas J.

"Raccoons are our blood enemies," said Flip J, affably scratching the back of his head.

"You're just going to leave it there?" asked Hayworth.

"We'll leave it there for a little while, and we'll see if a bigger animal, a scavenger, comes along and eats it," said Thomas J.

"Sure. It's no big deal," said Flip J. Blinking, he turned his kind face towards Hayworth.

"I asked you not to, that's all," said Hayworth. The rum turned in her stomach.

"I'm tired of this. Let's have a race," said Thomas J, to clear the air. "What should we race to, Hayworth?"

"Shut up, Thomas," said Hayworth.

"Come on, Hayworth, let's race," said Flip J. His sausage lips peeled back uncertainly. He scratched the back of his head again. He looked between the two of them.

"You choose the course, Hayworth," said Thomas J.

"I told you I want you to shut up, please," said Hayworth. They waited for her. She said, "We'll race a mile back through the woods until we get to the white boulder. Then we'll race back."

"Shortcuts?" asked Thomas J.

"Alright," said Hayworth.

"First one back to the dead raccoon wins," said Thomas J. He went off running, his red trunks flashing between the pale ash trees. Hayworth and Flip J. took after him, keeping to the path. Hayworth thought of Geronimo, but Flip J. wanted to talk.

"Hayworth," he loped alongside her, taking one stride for every two of hers, "do you believe that people could run as fast as horses?"

"Yes, I believe that," said Hayworth, loving him. "Why did you kill that raccoon?"

"It was sneaking around too much, and anyway what makes you think it was my bullet, and not Thomas J's?"

"You shot that raccoon, Flip J," said Hayworth, "and now you're just going to let it lie there."

"Raccoons die all the time," said Flip J, "but I don't want you to feel bad. Do you think Thomas J. protects you enough?"

"No. He believes I can stand up for myself."

"He lets you drink rum and water with us on the stoop," Flip J. observed.

"What is it like for you and Thomas J. to be best friends?" asked Hayworth.

"I love Thomas J." said Flip J, "Beyond that, it's like you might think." They ran on awhile.

"Do you think you're too old for me, Flip J?" asked Hayworth.

"Too old for what, Hayworth?"

"Don't be stupid, Flip J."

But Flip J. was not stupid. He had no guile. They ran on in silence, because they believed in feats of strength, and they wanted to beat Thomas J, and they wanted to beat each other. When they arrived at the white rock, Thomas J. had already marked it with a bit of charcoal, and was gone back through the trees. He must have taken the short cut because they hadn't met him on the path. Hayworth swung herself up onto the rock, with silver threaded through it. She pulled at the embroidery floss in her ears. "Well?" she asked. She leaned down towards Flip J. His teeth were sticky and gleaming through the dark.

No one knows what it's like for two boys to be best friends. We will always wonder what they talk about on long journeys when it's just the two of them, but we will never know because no one knows. It's a secret. We have to go by pieces. We know, for example, that it's nice to have a pal in your corner, and sometimes you don't even have to talk about it. Sometimes, if you get in a fight, you can just go off into the woods together and box it out. You don't have to talk about it, you just box it out, back in the thin ash woods, back by the raccoon hide-out, where the raccoons wash their stolen food in pools of water, those bandits, those aristocrats.

Flip J. put his head up, and Hayworth leaned down, and they kissed like two animals. They tasted each other, the tar-like liquor they'd been drinking, and the taste of running fast through the woods so your lungs open up. Then Hayworth jumped down from the rock and ran back through the woods, and she left Flip J. behind.

When she came back to the dead raccoon, Thomas J. sat on the stoop, breathing.

"Where's Flip J?" he asked, "Third place to a seventeen-year-old girl. Too bad."

"He let me win," said Hayworth. She knelt by the raccoon. It looked like it was leaping. Hayworth put her hand into its dull fur. It was still a bit warmer than the air around it. Its black paws were splayed. The bullet had gone in at the shoulder, and the shoulder was torn.

"You're not still upset about that raccoon, are you?" asked Thomas J.

"I'm going to skin it," said Hayworth.

"You don't know how to skin a raccoon."

"Lend me your knife."

Thomas J. came forward unsteadily from all the rum. He gave Hayworth his long knife, which was dull from him practicing throwing it, and it thunking into rotten wood.

Hayworth hefted the raccoon by its tail, but it was heavier than she'd expected, so she sank it back down into the intersection. Its head fell back, its mouth came open, and its teeth were a snarl of needles, useless. Hayworth turned the raccoon on its back. It was a boy raccoon. What Thomas J. had said was true. She didn't know how to skin it. She had never even considered skinning anything in the city that they came from.

Hayworth began between the hind legs with the knife. The blade punctured through the fur and skin easily, slishing inside, but when she turned the blade to pull it upwards towards the chin, she had to use all her strength, she had to use the knife like a saw, and the flesh and fur became ragged. Hayworth opened the raccoon. The stomach slid out onto the ground, a gummy pink sack, dragging a soft heap of intestines. The liver was blue. The kidneys, one after the other, Hayworth held in her hand. Each part was perfect, intact, a neat slick collection, tucked away.

She began to relish the searching knife, the gooey ordered work of it, she cut all the way up to the neck. Hayworth filled her hands with the fur, deep, filthy, and soft, with the layer of long hair skimming over the top, coarse and black tipped. At first the pelt peeled easily back, falling in a heavy fluid fold, but working the skin away from the leg bones stopped her. She had to scrape and scrape with the knife, but still the legs held steadily to their scraps of fur. Hayworth began to feel the night's heat. It started to stink a bit. Hair caked the dull knife.

Thomas J. sat on the storefront steps and sipped rum and water, watching and then not watching Hayworth's progress.

"I don't care about this," he told her. "I don't want to know anything about this. I think we should leave it alone."

"Do we have any salt?" she asked him.

"Salt?"

"I think I should pack the pelt in salt to cure it. Look in the five and dime and see if there's salt."

"I don't want to go in that five and dime all alone without a light," said Thomas J. "Where's Flip J, anyway?"

"I'd have expected him back by now," said Hayworth, looking into the woods.

"I don't like to go around in the dark alone," said Thomas J. "I wish Flip J. would come back."

But Flip J. had left the path to cut through the ash wood, and he caught his foot on a root, and he fell down and hit his head, and he had a long dream, and when he woke up, the moon shone through the trees just like milky daytime. Flip J. turned his head and came nose to nose with a doe's skull, its empty eyes wide with sympathy. He drew himself up to one elbow until he could see that he lay in a dark valley full of tumbling brown leaves. He wasn't lying on any actual ground, just on those shifting leaves, and bumping up underneath the heaps of leaves were skulls, deer skulls, piles of them. They emerged from beneath the valley as if washed to shore. The spindly wood was silent, and it let go a prickly sweet smell that ran all through Flip J. He put his head back down and looked up through the trees at the bright sky. He thought of kissing Hayworth, of how soft-hearted and smart-alecky she was. That's what we think he thought of. That's what we would have been thinking if we had been Flip J, but he was inscrutable and content.

Hayworth left the raccoon and came to sit with Thomas J.

"Wasn't he right behind you?" asked Thomas J, looking hard at her.

"If he's not back soon, we'll go find him," said Hayworth. She put her sticky hand on Thomas J's shoulder.

They waited in the dark on the stoop. A scavenger, a dark animal came sniffing into the intersection towards the raccoon carcass. It was another raccoon. It snuffled and nibbled at the dead raccoon.

"We'll wait for one more minute, and then we'll go look for him," said Hayworth.

"I don't like going around in the dark without him, that's all," said Thomas J.

* * *

They waited and waited for Flip J, who'd had a vision. When he came wandering back, blinking into the intersection, they held him and petted him, they clapped him on the back.

Convalescence

Frank Roger

The man opened his eyes and his first thought was: What the hell.

He looked around and took stock of his situation. He was in a hospital bed, and there was no one else around. He felt all right and wasn't hooked up to any medical equipment, so what was he doing here?

Wait a minute, he thought. There is something wrong with me. Who am I? What's my name? What happened to me, why am I here?

There were no answers to these questions. That wasn't normal. It might explain why he was here. He must have caught a disease or suffered an accident that wiped his memory.

A nurse entered the room and shot him a warm smile. "Good to see you're awake. How do you feel?"

The nurse's face wasn't familiar. Either he had never seen her before, or this too was a result of his loss of memory.

"I feel okay. Something's bothering me, though. I can't seem to remember anything. I even forgot my name."

"Don't worry, it's perfectly normal in your condition. Your memory should start coming back now."

"Can you tell me what happened to me?"

"The doctor will tell you everything you need to know. He'll come around later today. I'm sure everything will be all right."

She checked his pulse and his temperature, told him once more everything was fine and there was absolutely nothing to worry about, and left with the words, "I'll be back in a few minutes."

He shook his head. How could he not worry about his situation: was waking up in a hospital bed without any memories at all supposed to be reassuring?

He sat upright, unbuttoned his pyjamas and looked at his body. There were no scars visible, so he hadn't been operated. He checked for missing body parts, but nothing had been amputated. How silly, he thought, glancing at your legs and arms to be sure nothing's gone. Just to be on the safe side, he pulled down his pants too. Everything was okay down there as well. What a relief!

He walked over to the window and looked outside. His room was on the first floor of a five storey building. He saw nothing that provided him with a clue about his whereabouts: a grey sky, a lawn, lined with trees, houses in the distance. He could be anywhere.

Wasn't there something in the room that would enable him to identify himself? He was about to start his round of inspection as the nurse came in again, carrying a tray with his breakfast. Or was it his lunch? What time of day was it?

"I can see you're up and running," she said. "You seem to be doing fine. There you are. Enjoy your meal."

"Thank you. By the way, when can I see the doctor?"

"He's very busy right now, but he'll probably drop by in the afternoon."

"I'd like to know who I am and what happened to me. My memory is completely gone, you see. Really, this is extremely embarrassing."

"I understand, believe me. Now eat your meal before it gets cold. The doctor will tell you everything you need to know. And why don't you take a look at your personal belongings in the wardrobe over there. That might refresh your memory. Now if you'll excuse me, I have other patients to attend to."

"Fine."

The smell of the food made him aware of a gnawing hunger, so he sat down and wolfed down his meal: an indefinable clump of meat, peas, and mashed potatoes. Not quite a five-star course, but it did the job. He downed a glass of water, and went for the wardrobe.

His personal belongings consisted of a set of clothes. He rummaged through the pockets of the trousers and the coat, and found a wallet. Ah, he thought, we're finally getting somewhere. He produced a few banknotes and an ID.

The picture in the ID showed a face he was not familiar with. Was that his face? Did he look like that? He hurried to the bathroom and looked in the mirror. Yes, it was him all right. How strange that he didn't even remember what he looked like. He glanced at the name on the ID: Bob Smith. What a terribly common name. Was he really called Bob Smith? The name didn't even ring a bell. He was disappointed, as if he deemed himself entitled to a more classy name.

What else was there? His date of birth, 1978, which did not allow him to determine how old he was. His address: 77 Heybourne Street, Shepherd's Cross. Still no bells were ringing. Did he live there alone, was he married, did he have children? So now he knew who he was, at least in theory, for actually he still didn't have a clue about his identity and what had happened to him. If it hadn't been for the picture of the guy that just had to be him…

His belongings didn't yield any more information. He sat down on the bed and tried to remember, but nothing came.

* * *

He must have fallen asleep, because when he opened his eyes again he was back in his bed and saw the light of the rising sun coming in. His memory still hadn't come back, even if he knew his name now. Bob Jones, right? The name he had discovered yesterday on his driver's license. So he remembered what had happened yesterday. He was making some progress. His short term memory seemed to be working perfectly. But apart from his name, he still didn't know anything about himself.

The nurse he had already seen yesterday came in and said: "Oh, you're awake again. Did you sleep well?"

"Yes, I did. Why didn't the doctor come?"

"He did, but you were sound asleep and he preferred not to wake you up. He's not here today, but yesterday he did some final tests and decided that you've recovered completely. So you can go home in the afternoon. Isn't that good news?"

"I suppose it is," he said. "But wait a second. My recovery isn't complete. My memory still hasn't come back. I don't know who I am, what happened to me, how I ended up here ..."

"You shouldn't worry about all that. Your memory will come back gradually. There's just no need for you to stay here. This last phase of your recovery can easily be taken care of at home, where your family will help you. You'll be more comfortable there. Really, you shouldn't worry. You'll be back in shape soon enough."

"I've seen my address but I don't really know where I live," he protested. "I have no idea how to get there."

"Don't worry," she repeated. "We'll provide transport for you. Take it easy. Everything will be fine."

"So what do I do?"

"I'll bring you your breakfast, and afterwards you can put on your clothes. As soon as the paperwork is dealt with, you can go home."

He sighed. "Fine then. I suppose this is good news, but that's not how it feels to me. Still ..."

"There's no reason why you should stay here. As I said, you'll recover at home more comfortably. Now, if you'll excuse me."

He didn't wait for breakfast to put on his clothes. Is all this normal, he wondered. Being dismissed from a hospital with your memory missing, and without even seeing a doctor? Is all this really happening, or is it just a bad dream? What if I made a phone call to … well, to whom? He didn't have any names or phone numbers of relatives or friends, so his options were pretty limited. He finally got his breakfast, and shortly afterwards the nurse reappeared, accompanied by a man. She must have noticed his unease and impatience, and said:

"Johnny here will drive you home. We'll be in touch with you. Even if you're physically in perfect condition, the doctor will check your overall progress until he's sure your recovery is complete."

"You mean until my memory has come back?"

The nurse nodded. "Don't worry, you'll be fine. Now, please follow Johnny. Take care."

They left the room, and he glanced at the number on the door: 107. He followed Johnny down the corridor, past a large room where people were watching TV, and into the elevator. On the ground floor he threw a glance in the cafeteria, where a number of visitors were drinking coffee and talking. As they crossed the parking lot, he looked around. In front of the entrance was a small garden with a pond and half a dozen bronze statues. He rather liked the view. It had an element of romance to it. Before he got into the car, he looked at the hospital's name on the facade: Oak Ridge County Medical Institute. The name didn't ring a bell. Oak Ridge County? Was that where they were now, was this the place where he lived?

They left the parking lot, drove down a short stretch of road, across a bridge over a small river and finally arrived in the outskirts of a town.

Johnny, who had until now remained silent, suddenly said: "Are you okay? How long have you been at the hospital?"

"Frankly, I don't know," he said. "You see, my memory has gone, and although they told me it would come back, I still don't recall a thing. Nothing really. Nothing at all."

"That's funny," Johnny said. "Still, they let you go, so you must be all right."

"Maybe so, but that's not how I feel. My mind is like a blank page, you know what I mean?"

Johnny chuckled. "Oh yeah. That typical Monday morning feeling." He relapsed into silence and drove the car through boulevards and side streets, obviously knowing where he was heading. Finally he pulled over and pointed at a house, saying:

"Here we are, Heybourne Street. And there's number 77. That's where you live, right? Well, I hope they're expecting you. Goodbye."

"Goodbye." He got out and looked around. He didn't remember this street or the neighbourhood. Johnny didn't wait and drove off, leaving him alone in these unfamiliar surroundings. He reached into his pockets but didn't find a key. What the hell, he thought. I'll just have to ring the bell and hope somebody's home. Somebody who knows me and is expecting me.

He rang the bell and was relieved when a woman opened the door. Was this cute young chick his wife? He shot her a warm smile, hoping she would recognise him and tell him to come in, but she just stared and said: "Yes?"

"I'm back," he said. "They let me go. The hospital, I mean. I suppose you are … my wife, or perhaps …"

"I beg your pardon?" the woman asked, flabbergasted.

"Don't you know me?" he said, trying to hide the encroaching despair taking possession of him. "At the hospital they told me this was where I live. Now this may sound very strange, but I must have had an accident or a disease, you see, and my memory…"

The woman closed the door. He stood there panting for a few moments, fighting the chill that was spreading through his body. This wasn't going according to plan. He rang the bell again, and again, but the woman didn't open the door anymore. He checked the number on the bell, 77, which was correct. He also checked the name, but it wasn't his.

Had they made a mistake at the hospital? But this address did correspond with the one on his ID. There just had to be an explanation for this terrible misunderstanding. Just suppose his family had moved while he was at the hospital, and for some reason the guy doing the paperwork had failed to note the new address. In that case, the woman he had just seen was the new tenant, who obviously didn't know him. He had no idea how long ago his family had left, he didn't even know for how long he had been at the hospital. But how could he find his family's current address (if that was indeed the right explanation)? What should he do next?

Wait a second. If he had lived here until more or less recently, the neighbours might recognise him and offer some helpful information or advice. He rang the bell of number 75, but no one answered the door. He had more luck at number 79, where a tall black man appeared and said: "Yes?"

"Hi," he said, suddenly not quite sure how to present his case. "I wondered if you could help me. You see, I've been absent for a while, and I suffered memory problems, and they told me I used to live next door here, but your neighbour didn't seem to know me, and ..." His voice trailed off. He realised his story didn't make sense and this guy would probably think he was some kind of nut.

"I don't know what your problem is," the man replied gently, "but I've lived here for more than fifteen years and I've never seen you before, so I doubt you used to live here."

"But that means ..." He shook his head, unable to accept the consequences of what he was told.

"I'm afraid I can't help you," the black man continued. "But I suggest you go to the pub down the road here. It's that way." He pointed to the right. "Have a drink, calm down and talk to the bartender about your problem. He may be able to help you. Good luck, pal."

"Thank you."

The man shot him a smile and closed the door. The sinking feeling that had almost brought him to his knees on discovering he had probably never lived here made way for a faint ray of hope. Maybe he should follow this guy's advice, have a coffee and discuss his problem with the bartender.

He walked down the street until he arrived at the Rhythm & Booze, went in and ordered a coffee. There were only a few customers at this hour, so it wasn't too difficult to attract the bartender's attention. He realised he should tell a more coherent version of his story than he had used on the black man, or the effort would be lost.

"I was wondering if you could help me."

"What's your problem?"

"Well, you see, I was just released from the hospital, where I spent some time after an accident. I've recovered now, but I'm still suffering memory problems. I was told I used to live here in the neighbourhood, so I was hoping you might know me and fill me in on some of the missing details."

The bartender took a good look at him and shook his head. "I don't remember seeing you around here, so I doubt you used to live here. And I'm afraid your story doesn't make sense. I've definitely got the feeling you should still be in the hospital. Someone there made a mistake, you shouldn't have been released, or perhaps they mixed you up with another patient. No doubt they're overworked and short on staff and there's a perfectly logical explanation for your problem. Why don't you simply go back to the hospital to sort things out? I can call you a taxi if you want."

He nodded. "Yes, please. Call me a taxi." As a matter of fact, this was a good piece of advice. Why hadn't he thought of that himself? He finished his coffee and waited for his taxi.

As the car arrived he thanked the bartender, paid, and left. He got in and told the driver: "Take me to the Oak Ridge County Medical Institute."

The driver laughed and said: "You're joking, right?"

"No, I wasn't," he replied. The sinking feeling came back. This wasn't going as hoped. "Why did you think so?"

"Why would you go to that place?"

"I just have to be there."

"Well all right," the driver said. "If you insist. After all, it's your money."

"What's wrong with that hospital?"

The driver chuckled. "You'll see."

As they drove off he wondered why the driver had reacted this way. Did the hospital have a sinister reputation? The bartender wouldn't have made his suggestion if it was better to stay away from that place for whatever reason. But then again, had he mentioned the hospital's name to him? Hadn't he simply talked about "the hospital"? In that case the bartender couldn't have known he was talking about this particular place. Damned, things definitely weren't going right. The sinking feeling was growing stronger by the minute.

He looked out the window and noticed they were driving through a neighbourhood that seemed deserted. Not a living soul could be seen, nor any other vehicles. Most houses were in bad shape and appeared uninhabited, as if this part of the city had turned into a ghost town. He didn't recall passing through here earlier this morning, so he asked the driver:

"Are we going in the right direction? I don't think I've been here before."

"There's only one way to the Institute. We'll be there in a second. I still don't understand what you'll be doing there, but that's none of my business, I suppose."

The car finally crossed the bridge over the river and stopped in front of the hospital's entrance. He stared at it in utter disbelief.

"Well," the driver said, "here we are. You're sure this is where you want to be?"

I must be dreaming, he thought. The garden and the pond were overgrown with plants and shrubs, a miniature jungle, untended for many years. The statues were gone, only their bases could be seen, encrusted with vegetation as well. The hospital itself was in ruins, and must have been for quite some time. Its doors and windows were shattered, parts of the upper storeys had collapsed. Yet he still recognised the building he had left this morning. He could even see its name in faded letters above the entrance. This was indeed the place where he had stayed until a few hours ago—but it couldn't have crumbled away in such a short time. What the hell was going on here?

He turned to the driver and said hoarsely: "This place is ... abandoned ..."

"That's about the least you can say."

"Do you know when it closed down?"

"I'm not sure, but that must have been quite a while ago."

Should he tell the driver that he had been released here just a few hours ago, and that the hospital was still a normally functioning one when he left? How could he possibly expect the guy to believe him? He would think his passenger had lost his mind. So maybe it was better not to say anything.

"I'd like to take a look inside," he said. "Wait here, please. I won't be long."

"Inside? What do you expect to find in there? Not medical care, I hope."

"I just need to take a look inside. I'll be right back."

He got out of the car and walked through the open door. The shards of glass the ground was covered with crunched under his feet. He cast a glance over his shoulder, noticed that the driver was waiting patiently. He was confident that he wouldn't drive off, as he hadn't been paid yet. Still, he wouldn't put the guy's patience to the test and keep his round of inspection short.

He carefully made his way around the debris littering the floor and walked past the cafeteria, now a complete shambles, with what was left of the furniture swept aside in a corner. No one had drunk a coffee here for some time. He stopped before the elevator, and couldn't refrain from pushing the button. Nothing happened. How strange, he thought, chuckling. That thing still worked earlier this morning. Although it definitely looks as if it hasn't worked for a long time.

Well, now that I'm here, why don't I take a look at my old room, he said. He went up the flight of stairs leading to the first floor. The climb was quite tricky, as the steps were in poor condition and there was lots of rubbish all over the place. On top of that, it was also pretty dark where no light from outside came in. He made it safely to the first floor and walked down the corridor, past the room where people had been watching TV. The room was now stripped of its TV and its audience.

A bit further down he stopped in front of his own room. The number 107 was still faintly visible. He walked in, looked around. This had been his room all right. How much time had he spent here? And what had happened to him in this hospital, what had happened to the hospital itself for that matter? His bed was gone, his wardrobe reduced to a skeleton of rotting wood.

He went over to the window and looked out. This was indeed the view that he remembered. He shook his head. It all felt so unreal. The whole situation, everything that had happened since he woke up in this very room, in the bed that had been over there. Being released here without seeing a doctor, his loss of memory, his home address that didn't prove correct, and now this, the hospital that had changed beyond recognition in a few hours' time. Was he dreaming all this? Was this just a terrible nightmare he would suddenly wake up from?

I have to go back now, he thought. I can't let that taxi driver wait there for too long. He left his room, for the second time today, went down the stairs and hurried to the exit. He stopped dead in his tracks when he noticed the taxi was no longer there.

Why did the guy leave him stranded here? He hadn't been inside the hospital for that long. And he had gone off without being paid. Now that was unusual.

This meant of course that he would have to walk back to the city. He realised he didn't really have a place to go to, but staying here at the ruined hospital was definitely not an option. He would try a police station, they should be able to help him. So he set off, and for some reason he quickened his pace, as if he knew time was running out and he had better hurry.

He ran until he reached the river, and howled with rage as he saw the bridge had gone. He shook his fists at his unseen enemy, stared at the remnants of the bridge that could still be seen in the water. This was impossible. He had crossed the river mere minutes ago. It was as if time had speeded up at this place, and when he returned after ten minutes had passed for him, over here ten years had gone by.

Could that perhaps explain why the driver had left? Maybe the guy had waited patiently for an hour or more, wondering where his passenger had gone to. Maybe he had looked for him, and had finally left in despair, perhaps furious because he hadn't been paid. So that might be the explanation for his bizarre adventures: time was going faster in some places than in others, leaving the whole world out of joint.

But that theory didn't explain everything. His loss of memory, for instance, or his release from the hospital before his full recovery, or his home address where he had never lived. What was the address again? And what was his name? How strange that he should forget these things. This meant he was not recovering at all, his condition was even deteriorating. He reached into his pocket, took his ID to check his name and address again.

The brittle and yellowed document crumbled to pieces in his hands, as if the paper had failed to withstand the ages it had spent in his pocket. He stared at the shreds of paper on the ground, like petals of a withered flower crushed by a gust of wind.

Hey, he thought, I think I'm beginning to understand. This breakdown… the hospital, the bridge, the document… It's also happening to me. I don't know how or why, I have no idea who or what is causing it and for what purpose, if there is one at all, but I'm sure I'm the victim of the same phenomenon that's making everything decay here.

He shook his head, trying to clear it of these unsavoury thoughts. There's no point in wallowing in my bad luck, he thought. I shouldn't give in to these dark feelings, I'd better face the situation and make the best of it. Why am I hanging around here at the river that I can't cross anymore? Wouldn't it be better to return to the…

To the what? Where had he come from? He had been running until he reached the river, but he no longer remembered where he had come from. Nor did he remember his name. He kicked at the scraps of paper at his feet. Wasn't there something about them that had attracted his attention? He sighed, cursed his loss of memory. Who was he, where was he, what was he doing here?

There were no answers. He shrugged, and walked back down the road he must have come from. I'll find out where I was running from, he thought. I'll see where I end up.

He kept walking but arrived nowhere. The road dwindled into a path, and the path suddenly stopped. It didn't lead to anything. He was lost. He turned around and started walking back, but couldn't find any trace of the path or the road anymore. All around him there was just a desolate landscape, a barren waste of dirt and stones.

I'm lost, he thought. Completely lost. My memory has gone and so has all the rest. There's no point in going any further. There's nothing out there, neither in front of me nor behind me.

I'm lost. Lost? What did that mean? Hadn't it always been like this? Had there ever been something else? He concentrated, but couldn't recall the problem that was bothering him. His mind was a blank, a mental mirror image of the landscape surrounding him.

There was nothing, neither in his mind nor in the outside world. Fine, he thought. I assume this is a normal situation. Let's simply accept it as it is then.

A smile appeared on his face as his eyes roamed the vast expanse of wasteland.

Nothing. Nothing at all.

His smile vanished as he discovered he was beginning to fade, and his last thought was: What the hell …

Fixing the Picture

Regina Edwards

It had just gone seven when the cat jumped up onto my bonnet and stared at me through the windscreen, eyes narrowed. *It won't happen tonight, Livy,* it seemed to say. *Go Home.* One honk of the horn sent it darting off. I was on a mission and would be spending most of the evening sitting in my old V-Dub.

There had been a time when I thought I'd never own a car. Cycling around the hills of St Lucia kept me toned and suited my student budget. *Bikes are the way to go,* Riley had convinced me. *Good for the environment and the most it'll ever cost us is a new front wheel.* We rode everywhere, poor but happy. When things changed, I inherited my grandmother's Volkswagen.

Myrtle had recently turned twenty and in car years was in the throes of menopause—moody clutch, jammed odometer, and she kept overheating. Still, we'd been through a lot together, and I couldn't bring myself to let her go.

"Come on, old girl." I popped an olive into my mouth, foraged from the Deli Cafe at Gailey Fiveways. "Headlights peeled. See anything yet?"

"Blister in the Sun" whispered from the car radio. I also had my iPod, weighed down with songs for when the almost inevitable eventuated. Music, I found, worked like a T3 lane for the emotions. I was watching the road when my mobile vibrated in my lap. Jerking up as if tasered, I checked the caller ID: Alex, my housemate. Fleeting annoyance. I had been concentrating.

"Hello."

"Hey Livy, it's me."

"Yes, I know."

"Where are you?"

"Taringa."

"Oh, Westerham Street?"

"Where else …"

"Do you think you could give it a miss this week?"

"Why's that?"

"Vlad's here."

"As in Viagra Vlad?"

"That's the one. He's down from Nambour for the weekend. He'd love to catch up with you."

Alex had an impressive stack of ex-boyfriends. Unconscious of her natural beauty, she failed to fathom why men swarmed around her like worker bees. The collective, incessant buzz of excitement took on the form of a theme park, and Alex treated each relationship as a ride. She met Vladimir Porkhomovsky at a U.Q. Engineering ball, their inauspicious union born out of alcohol-induced misjudgement. Inexplicably, it lasted two years.

"Surely you mean 'you.'"

"What?"

"You mean he'd like to catch up with *you.*"

"Whatever. You know what I mean. I thought we could have a few quiet drinks."

Or I could just whack myself over the head with a month-old carrot, I thought.

"You know I'm"—I struggled for the right word—"occupied."

"Oh for God's sake, Olivia. It's a perfectly good Friday and you're marinating in your stinky beetle. Come and be normal for a change. Please!"

The dig at Myrtle was low. Admittedly, she did leak when it rained, and for weeks after harboured a sinister odor, but still ...

A scrub turkey twitched its head at me as it meandered past. *Don't go*, it said.

"It's Friday, Alex. I can't."

"Why not?"

If I told her, she wouldn't believe me.

"Sure you can. Start the engine. Drive home. Doctor's orders."

I felt cornered inside my own car, and made an indecipherable noise.

"I'll see you soon, okay?" Alex hung up.

I glared at my phone. "She's going to keep calling me, and calling me ..."

Tonight, the moon was going Full Frontal. I spotted a flying fox draped like laundry over a power line—fairly common around here. Crickets were in the throes of something morbidly unmusical: "Requiem for a Fruit Bat," perhaps.

Brisbane summer. The air had been pregnant with rain all afternoon and now the first drops were being delivered. Another scrub turkey bolted into the foliage.

I turned my head to take one last look at the block of flats. They seemed the same as in 2002. The rain made me edgy and I knew I wanted to stay. But then there was Alex. *Come up higher and ski down the blue runs,* she'd said at Thredbo. *You'll be all over this in no time.* And in no time at all I was nearly all over the snow. Alex was Uri Geller and I was her spoon.

Reluctantly, I started the engine.

* * *

We lived in a house nestled in Chapel Hill. It was a 1970s two-storey cavity brick fortress that we rented from Myron—an obstreperous old Greek. His house was his temple and he reminded us of this monthly, driving by unannounced and complaining that the garden bed was overgrown or that the tomato vine needed spraying. We suspected this violated our rights as tenants. There were three highly fertile mango trees in the front yard, and although we had to share our fruit with the flying foxes, there was still enough to last us and everyone we knew throughout summer. It compensated for Myron's recurring raids.

The garage was blocked by a spiffy red convertible. I somehow couldn't assimilate this with the old Vlad. Always in flannie and thongs (before they became a fashion statement), Vlad used to trundle around Brisbane in an old station wagon. An exotic cocktail of clothes, tapes, tools, bits of computer hardware, and textbooks invariably filled the boot and back seat. Where was Vlad hoarding his junk now?

Riley wasn't into 'things'. I thought back to our little flat. *Four plates, four knives, four forks. One print on the wall. We are minimalists,* he used to say to me, about us.

Eyeing the convertible, I off-roaded to a spot under one of the mango trees. It was perverse. The risks were obvious: exploded half-eaten mango on the bonnet. Bat poo. With drought and water restrictions, I would make excuses not to clean it.

Inside, Vlad and Alex were sitting at the dining table. Alex was sipping a glass of water while Vlad cradled a can of Ginger Ale. There was no beer in sight.

Vlad stood up to greet me. Memorable teeth, big and crooked. Hair had thinned a bit. No traces of acne left, though, and he'd always had good facial structure.

Vlad lurched towards me with long, open arms, but I was still holding my tub of olives. Not knowing which way to commit, he gave me a half handshake and half peck, which cancelled each other out.

"Olivia Harrington—how delightful to see you again!" A second generation Australian, Vladimir Porkhomovsky was raised on borsch and *Blackadder*. He always addressed me in a mock British voice, a passive dig at my hoity surname. It suggested I might have grown up with ponies, whereas I never even had a Cabbage Patch doll.

Undoubtedly nicer to see me last time, I thought, *given that I was two sizes smaller then.*

Alex's presence always fuelled my body paranoia, her alluring behind a peach to my pear.

"Take a seat, Liv." Alex straightened her long leg, pushing a chair out for me. The table was littered with corn chips, a half-eaten cheese, keys, mobiles, lighter, and cigarettes.

"Thanks." I sat down, imagining a perfectly round peach dropping and bouncing, and alongside it a pear—no bounce, just a thud and then a slump, looking sad and inedible.

Vlad spread some brie on a corn chip. "Bandicoot and I were just discussing the grim economic times."

I've never known why Vlad calls Alex 'Bandicoot'. *Randy Bandy?*

"She says Capitalism is failing." Vlad pointed an accusing finger and jammed three Doritos into his mouth. "She sounds like Neapolitan the Pig!"

Vlad was never known for his attention to detail. Alex furrowed her brow and laughed. "*Neapolitan!* All I said was that countries with socialist leanings—like Sweden and Finland— have a high standard of living."

"Yes, but the government takes half their money!" Vlad turned to me, profoundly earnest. "I tell you—Communism works in theory but not in practice."

If I were a cat, all my hair would have stood on end. Alex cast me a surreptitious smile, knowing how much I loathe this phrase. It suffers from so much overuse. But this is what people do—clump together second-hand thoughts and half-digested ideas, fashionable phrases. They swallow everything and cough it back up like hairballs. Vlad read little but put a lot of faith in Orwell—his understanding of communism no more than a pig in a poke.

"So anyway. How have you been, Olivia?"

I smiled and nodded reassuringly, having just slipped an olive into my mouth. "Still seeing that philosophy student?"

He was referring to Riley. Alex obviously hadn't told him anything.

"Environmental Science. Not Philosophy." And with that I fled to the kitchen and helped myself to a glass of cask white.

"He seemed like a nice guy," Vlad called. "Never wore any shoes …"

Riley believed that humans hadn't evolved to wear shoes; that shoes interfered with the natural spring of the sole.

"Thought they were bad for his feet." I sat back down, crossing my legs.

Vlad crunched noisily. "Shoes bad for feet, hey. Well, what about high heels?"

"He didn't wear those either."

Alex laughed. Vlad joined in, belatedly. "Did you end up finishing your Engineering degree?"

"No, I got side-tracked." I frowned at my wine. "I went overseas, did the London work-travel thing." Temping in Hammersmith and making barely enough money to cover rent, food and Jacob's Creek Shiraz. "And you?" I deflected.

"I didn't finish either." There was no remorse in his voice. "I look after old buggerers now."

Alex's cheeks bulged around a mouthful of water. "Oh dear," I said.

"Buggers! I meant old *buggers*!"

"The elderly," Alex clarified.

"Yes, there are a lot of old people in Nambour for some reason."

So Vlad's in aged care, I thought. *What a hoot.* This was the same person who gave Viagra to a golden retriever; who attended a lecture with a live fish in his pants; who drove cane toads into the Forgan Smith Building with a 4-iron. What Alex perceived as a zest for life, I saw as a complete disregard for it.

"Excuse me." Suddenly, Vlad was on his feet. "Nicotine calls." Scooping up his cigarettes and phone, he wandered outside.

Alex and I sat and listened to fruit bats shrieking as they devoured mangoes from our trees. *Vampires*, I thought—as an image of a rabid-fanged bat with mango juice dripping from its face flashed through my mind.

"It's not his, you know," Alex whispered. "He's hired it for the weekend."

"It's not his what? Oh, the car."

As long as I'd known Alex, she'd loved everything that was considered high quality. Single malt whisky and Cuban cigars. Swiss watches, Gore-Tex raincoats. On some level she knew it was shallow, and perceiving it as a weakness, detested it in others.

"He thinks the car will impress you?"

Alex shrugged, smiling seductively. Naturally blonde strands of hair lay plastered across her forehead. It was humid in the house and we were sweating, despite the overzealous ceiling fan whirring above. We agreed not to tell Vlad about the Jag in the garage.

He returned, reeking of smoke. "Shall we go out for a drive, get some chow?"

I looked at Alex but she just shrugged. "I'm hungry."

I knew this would happen. Alex operated on partial information. I never saw the full picture until it was too late. Coffee at the Kuta Café would become a ten-kilometre hike around

Mt Coot-tha. A quick food-run to Woolies would turn into a day wasted at Westfield.

I wondered what was happening at Westerham Street, and what could have happened if I'd stayed.

"What about the quiet night in?"

"Bugger a quiet night in!" Vlad waved his arms around—an echo of his Russian heritage. "We'll paint the town purple! Come on, let's go for a spin."

"It's too hot tonight, Liv." Alex stood up. "I want to go somewhere with air-conditioning."

I was caught in a current of appetite and enthusiasm, and before I knew it was bundled into the back of a car intended for two—the rear seat merely a pretence.

As we drove along Moggill Road, I wondered where we were headed. If it had been my choice I would have picked the Schonell Pizza Café. I love the simplicity of ordering a letter of the alphabet. But, given Vlad's need to impress, I suspected we would be going to a place where the price and size of the meal are inversely proportional. I call such restaurants 'red holes' because they suck up money and keep people in the red.

"Damn rain! I really wanted to have the roof down." Vlad sounded apologetic, as if anyone cared. Gazing out through the drizzle, I soaked up the city lights.

* * *

We pulled into the Emporium complex in the Valley. I observed the metro set moving about. The women made me feel underdressed with their frocks, foils, makeup, and stilettos. I was resigned to being a dag in my currently outdated flare-cut jeans.

Vlad lead us into the Belle Epoch. The inside was impressive. The distinctly antiquated decor spoke of another time, another place. We were in the Valley but could just as easily have been in Montparnasse, Paris.

A waitress with short dark hair approached. "Good evening. A table for three?" She had a heavy French accent.

My awe at the surroundings turned to embarrassment as Vlad put an arm around each of us and grinned. "Oui, un tableau pour trois, er, please."

"Do you have a réservation?"

"Yes, under 'Bond.'"

Oh, good god. I had an unfortunate flash of Daniel Craig with a fish wiggling in his pants.

We were lead across mosaic tiles to a booth with plump red vinyl seats. Alex sat closest to the lantern, its glow capturing her low-cut silk blouse. The walls were panelled with mirrors that had been rusted around the edges. I felt that I had neither the finance nor the plumage for a place like this.

A dreamy, barely comprehensible young waiter floated by to tell us about the specials.

"I'll have the grilled scallops and the seafood platter." Alex always went for seafood.

"I'll have the fooey grass, thanks, and the special, please—the 'shat-on Breanne.'" Vlad chronically mispronounced the two most expensive dishes on offer.

"The Chateaubriand, sir, it is, er, for two, yes?"

Vlad took a moment to process. "That's alright. I'm quite hungry!" As if it were a delightful revelation.

The waiter turned his attention to me.

"I'll have the pumpkin velouté, please."

"And for main?"

"I'll have that as a main."

"The velouté, er, very small. I can do, er, main course size, yes?"

"No, just an entrée size, please."

"Okay." He shrugged, then scribbled on his notepad. Alex watched him as he left. Vlad leaned towards us.

"Don't you think he's overdoing the accent?"

"Vlad, he's French."

With sudden alarm, I realised we'd forgotten to order wine. "What about wine? Are we having wine?" But I could tell from their expressions they were intending to do France dry. Where was the spirit?

Alex rarely drank. Control was not something she liked to step away from. Vlad, I suspect, must have realised after a decade of embarrassing incidents that he really needed to be frugal with what little of it he had. They poured themselves some water. I ambushed a passing waitress and ordered myself half a litre of house red.

"Mmmmhhm!" Vlad made a noise mid-sip. "I've got it!" And spilled his water. Archimedes would have approved. "They're *not* French!"

"What?" Alex and I looked at him.

"How could you have so many French waiters, all in Brisbane?"

"Studying, probably." Alex flicked her hair. "There are a lot of international students in Brisbane, you know."

"Well I don't believe it." Vlad gave the table a friendly pound with his fist, and looked around suspiciously. "I think they're local hospitality graduates trained to speak in a French accent."

Alex laughed. "Vlad, you're a psycho!" But she said it as if it were a good thing.

Their entrées arrived and I got stuck into my wine.

"So, Olivia." Vlad impaled the entire serve of *foie gras* on his fork. "What's this secret stuff you get up to on Fridays?"

Damn her loose lips. Alex only knew that I drove to Westerham Street because I'd taken her along once, although on that particular night there had been nothing to see and Alex decided I was going batty.

Like jumping out of a window, I experienced a fleeting urge to tell them exactly what I had been doing, but thought better of it. "Don't the two of you have a lot to catch up on?"

"We've done a bit of that." Vlad cast a fond glance at Alex, who was deciding which scallop to stab first. "C'mon Livy, spill."

"I just go and park on the street where I used to live." It was my turn to be dealing out half-truths.

"Where you lived before moving in with Bandy?"

"No. Before London."

"Why?"

"I find it comforting."

Vlad looked to Alex for any warning signs, but her gaze was averted. And then, eureka again. "Oh! That's where you used to live with Riley. I remember now. So you're not together any-more, but ... he's not still living there is he?"

"No." Another half-truth.

"Well, Olivia." Vlad poached a scallop. "You need to move on. It's creepy to still be going to the old flat, you know?"

"Yes, I know."

"What's so special about this guy, anyway?" Vlad's wander-ing eye followed a passing waitress.

Because he was interested in truth. Because he took the time to understand things and form his own ideas. Because he cared about the world and wanted to make it a better place. Because ...

"... he wasn't like anybody else."

Our waiter materialised and cleared their entrée plates.

"Well, *I'm* not like anybody else. Face it, Livy H: everyone is unique. Everyone has something special to give." Clearly hun-gry, Vlad gawked at every main that was whizzed past. More borrowed words. *It's that sort of drivel that makes me miss Riley all the more.*

Vlad stood up, taking cigarettes out of his back pocket. "Sorry, girls. Just off for a quick cancer fix."

Moments after he left, our mains arrived. I studied my piti-ful velouté. Oversized bowl with a splash of something almost orange. I buried my face in my hands. "This was a bad idea, Alex. I should have stayed at Westerham Street."

"Not true." Alex tipped an oyster into her mouth. "You really need to quit this disturbing habit of yours. Mmm, these are fantastic."

"Do you think I've lost the plot?"

"No, not really. But I do think you need to stop living in the past."

I made figure eights in my pumpkin cream. "Why did you ask me to come tonight?"

"I thought it would be good for you. Better than wasting time in your car." Another oyster down the hatch. With three spoonfuls I ate my velouté.

"What did Vlad mean when he said you've already caught up?" I wasn't entirely sure I wanted to hear the answer, but Alex looked sheepish and my suspicions were confirmed. I helped myself to more wine. "I can't believe you haven't seen him for— what? eight years?—and the first thing you do is go to bed."

Alex shrugged, attacking a lobster. "Couch, actually."

"That was unnecessary."

"Sorry. The sex was always good, that's all."

"Whatever." I pinched a prawn from her platter. "I couldn't sleep with someone I didn't love."

"Germaine Greer would feel let down."

"Screw Germaine Greer."

"Maybe you should."

"What?"

"Maybe you *should* sleep with someone else. It might help you come to terms with what happened. Move on." She kept talking but the wine had risen to my head and I started to swim away.

Here I was, filling the space between two people who had nothing of substance to connect them. Everything for them was just passing the time—food; sex; conversation—and they had duped me into joining them.

"It's just escapism, Alex," I heard myself say.

"You're the one dousing yourself in alcohol ..."

I looked around at the fake mosaic tiled floor and the fake rusted mirrored walls. What only a short time ago had enchanted, suddenly made me sad. We'd left modern day Chapel Hill and ended up in 1900s Paris. It was a form of time travel. I wasn't the only one trying to elude the present.

Vlad returned, cigarette smell in tow, and sank his eyes into the lukewarm piece of cow in front of him.

I sculled the last of my wine. "Sorry, guys. I'm really tired." Depositing two twenties on the table, I stood up to leave.

"Where are you going?" Alex must have felt bad.

"Home. Have a good time, you two. I'll see you later."

Vlad looked confused, his attention wavering between me and his steak. Alex touched my arm.

"Livy, don't go." A token request. I was already moving.

Outside there was a pleasant breeze. Girls were still strutting around on heels—in pain, no doubt, but at least they were high. I wandered down Ann Street in search of a taxi.

* * *

My driver's name was Zaheer. Bollywood band fare filled the car—taunting me, as if somewhere else, someone was having a ball.

"Where would you like to go Ma'am?"

"Home, please."

"And where is that, Ma'am?"

"Westerham Street. Just off Indooroopilly Road." It wasn't my address anymore, but it was where I wanted to be. I wound the window all the way down.

As we turned onto Coronation Drive, I gazed at the river. The lights reflected in the water looked larger than usual. Or was it just the wine? I remembered cycling along the river in the middle of the night, loving the darkness and the feeling of the wind on my face.

"Have you had a good evening, Ma'am?"

"No, not really."

"Oh, why?" He looked young, mid-twenties maybe.

"Because I don't belong here."

"I beg your pardon?"

"Because I spent the night with my housemate and her ex-boyfriend, and they only wanted my company until they were ready to be alone again. I'm like the link that no one misses."

"Sounds complicated!" Zaheer laughed uncertainly. "You must have other friends, no?"

I thought about the people at work, brought together by circumstance—our interaction consisting almost entirely of jokes sent via email, even though we sit right next to each other. "All my friends have left town."

"Why?"

"I just make the kind of friends who never stay in one place for long."

"And your family?" Zaheer turned down the music.

"Scattered. None in Brisbane."

"Oh, that's no good." He made a sad face.

"Are you a student?" I asked.

"Yes. I am a student of life!" He laughed. "But I am also studying Engineering. Did you also come to Brisbane to study?"

"Partly, but mainly because of a boy." I surprised myself with that admission.

"Ah." Zaheer smiled, revealing big white teeth. "And where is the lucky man tonight?"

We had stopped at a traffic light in Toowong. Outside, it started to rain again. I felt as if the water would come through the car, and that I would melt like the witch in the Wizard of Oz.

"He's at Westerham Street." *Except he wasn't so lucky.*

Zaheer replied with something like, "Sounds like a bundle of happiness," but as we passed Sir Fred Schonell and turned onto Heroes Avenue, my head was rattling, memories like hail on the roof of the taxi.

—*Salad sandwiches at Perrin Park. One year, it floods. Riley and I, paddling waist deep in water. Southbank at night. A cat by the river's edge, bell ringing as it runs, slips. We watch it swim but there is no way back up. Riley doesn't care—cats kill native birds. Magpies swooping at Riley's head as he rides, but he refuses to wear a helmet. It's all a conspiracy. Compulsory helmeting so that corporations make more money. Life through the eyes of Riley—bad and beautiful at the same time. And then one Friday, the world becoming ugly. Cruel. Unbearable—*

We arrived. Paid and thanked, Zaheer drove off and I was standing alone on Westerham street.

The rain drew the smell of bitumen and vegetation into the air, and somewhere nearby some possums were making a creepy racket. The rain was a good sign. I walked slowly towards the block of flats and climbed the stairs. Quietly, I fetched the chair from the end of the walkway and placed it by the window. Standing on the chair, I rose up slowly until I could just see over the windowsill. The furniture was recognisably ours—the landlord hadn't changed it in seven years—but the print hanging on the wall was not. *They* have a picture of swans. A light was on in the study. That meant the girlfriend was still there—still waiting for him to come home.

I made my way back out to the street and sat at the bus shelter. Peering at my watch in the dark, I was surprised to see that it was almost a quarter to ten. *He's late tonight.*

My phone vibrated. An SMS from Alex.

[r u at home?]

I considered my reply.

[y. Don't worry.]

[k. c u soon]

I slumped back onto the seat and gazed up Indooroopilly Road, waiting.

Vlad will probably stay for the weekend. After he leaves, Brian will come back from Sydney and attach himself like a limpet. She'll probably leave him behind too.

There is something about this time, this place. The current is too strong. Nothing stays still long enough to take hold. Like a kaleidoscope, the pieces move, the picture ever-changing, each one real but only for an instant, and in that one instant everything can change.

I closed my eyes and remembered the picture that stayed still, that extended forward in time, year after year. It was meant to last forever. But, one Friday, the picture fell and broke, and now I was in the wrong time.

When I started coming to Westerham Street, it was to remember the time when the world felt more real to me. I wanted so much to go back and fix the picture, and then, one Friday, something remarkable happened—I was given that chance. If I focused on the picture hard enough, I found I could sometimes bring it back.

Time passed—half an hour perhaps—then I heard the bike. Opening my eyes, I jumped up to look. *Who will it be?* And I could hardly contain myself when I realised it was Riley! He flew down the hill, his afro mass of curly dark hair trailing like a cape. Not noticing me, he turned into the driveway and glided straight past to the base of the steps.

I waited a few minutes while he carried his bike upstairs and went inside. Moving the chair back to the window, I peeked in and looked at the print on the wall: *elephants! Not swans. Riley must have gone into the study to find me.* I waited quietly and could hear a faint murmur. Minutes later, we emerged into the kitchen, where I had a good view.

I was wearing my paisley print shirt from Lifeline. Riley retrieved some Woolies fruitcake from the fridge and cut it on a Pyrex plate. He recounted his day as he nibbled.

I looked into my eyes and saw an innocence that I had never recognised in my reflection as a youth. Even photos hadn't captured what I now saw, looking at a younger version of myself. Riley started to laugh at something that he'd said, his dark eyes full of life as I indulged him. He put the cake down and wrapped his arms around me, kissing my forehead. I knew I was tired and wanted to go to bed, but I always waited for Riley to come home from campus.

I thought about the time-switch and what caused it to take place. In the last six months it had happened only twice, on each occasion when the current tenant rode his bike home on a Friday night. I wondered whether this was the link—an identical action separated only by time. If he hadn't been so much like Riley, could I have willed myself back?

I kept watching us. Riley kissed me on my cheeks, my nose, and my lips. I held the kiss. It was difficult to be on the wrong side of the glass. But there I was, too heavy on my feet, standing on a chair and spying like some pervert on two people happy and in love. Such a version of me was never meant to exist. What I saw before me, this was a picture I needed to fix, quickly, before the fuse blew on my time-switch.

The first time I succeeded in flicking the time-switch, I was so stunned that I watched us right through dinner. I saw us wash up, read on the couch, walk in and out of the bathroom until we went to bed and turned out the lights. I listened to the murmur of us talking, then fell asleep on our doorstep. I woke up on *their* doorstep.

The second time, I mustered the courage to knock on the door, barely able to breathe as Riley walked towards me. But when the door opened, it was the current tenant who stood in front of me. The guy looked suitably puzzled when I mumbled something about the wrong address—the number five was huge and black on the bright orange door—and I stumbled away. *It is the right address. Just the wrong time.*

I thought perhaps that the time-switch allowed me to glimpse the past, but not vice versa, flicking off the instant I came face to face with Riley or my former self. But there had to be some way to fix the picture. I took the message for Riley out of my purse and read it one last time.

* * *

Please do not disregard this letter as a random act of madness. This is a warning from the future. Now, you are young and fearless, and think you are impervious to the world. You don't wear a bicycle helmet because you think only the corporations will benefit, but what if you're wrong?

It's a steep ride down from Gailey Fiveways. You should ride slower. Cars sometimes drive too quickly along Westerham Street and may not see you coming down the hill in the dark, especially in the rain. Take extra care on Fridays, when you ride home late.

I know your first reaction will be to laugh at this letter. But look at the girl you love. Can you imagine what life would be like for her if her perfect love were cut short, and she alone remained to carry the severed thread?

I know you are stubborn, I know you don't believe, but please do this one thing anyway, for her.

Olivia.

* * *

Taking a deep breath, I slipped the message under the door and tiptoed back down the stairs. Just as I reached the bus shelter, a black Jag came careering along Westerham Street. A frazzled Alex leaned over and rolled down the window.

"You loopey fruit loop. You said you'd gone home!"

"I did, sort of. I left a message for Riley." I felt calm, elated. "I think I've fixed the picture."

"What? Oh, good god. First you spend six months on a stakeout, now you've moved on to stalking. Wonderful. Now please get in the car."

There was no reason not to. We drove home in the rain.

"Why did you come for me?"

"Well, you weren't at Chapel Hill, so I thought to myself, *She's at her* other *home*, except tonight you don't have your car or even your olives."

"Where did you leave Vlad?"

"Vlad's catching the end of the football."

"I'm sorry if I made you worry."

Alex shook her head. "So, what did you write in this message of yours?"

"Just a warning."

"About?"

"About how things can get broken."

"You mean people?"

"Yes."

Alex sighed as quietly as she could and was silent for the rest of the journey.

* * *

As soon as we entered the front door, Alex disappeared upstairs. "Go and sit with Vlad. I'll be right down."

I plonked myself down on the couch. Vlad's eyes were glued to the TV but he spared me a look. "Hey, Olivia. You'll never believe it—the Bunnies are caning the Roosters..."

Little men ran all over the giant screen. Blue. Red. White. Green. Swarming around. Coming together and moving apart again. It meant nothing to me.

I heard the printer humming in the upstairs study, then footsteps creaking. Alex returned and gently placed an A4-printout on the coffee table. "It's about time you saw this, Liv."

My body went cold.

"This?" My voice faltered. "Where did you get this?"

"Mark."—*Policeman. Another ex.*—"I asked him to dig it up."

I had seen the picture once before, but it had been moving. There was a small but deep wound on the side of his forehead. Blood had run down and spattered over his cheeks, eyes and chin, forming a mosaic pattern. I reeled and fell back into that Friday.

It is dark, raining. I hear the car screech and the woman shrieking, hysterical. She's right outside our flat, runs straight towards me. Call an ambulance, she screams, on our driveway, but I run to the road. Riley with blood on his face. My world collapsing. I take off my shirt, try to stop the bleeding, but blood trickles from his nose and mouth. The rain, always washing it away. I can't stop the blood from moving.

"It was an accident, Liv. Riley was at the wrong place at the wrong time."

"Exactly." I looked at the photo. A broken Riley in a broken past. "But I've fixed this now."

"You can't fix it." Alex sat down and put her arm around me. "Riley died the instant that car hit him. That was seven years ago, Livy. You don't live at Westerham Street anymore."

Vlad muted the Bunnies and tactfully left the room. My eyes followed him as he walked to the kitchen. "You told him?"

"Only about the accident."

"But that's the thing, Alex—it wasn't just an accident. He wasn't wearing a helmet, and if he'd worn a helmet—"

"But he didn't, and you can't change what happened."

I turned to Alex and smiled. How could I make her understand, that tonight everything had changed, that there was now a place where the picture wasn't broken?

Vlad returned with a beer and fixed his eyes on me. He was trying very hard to look like a giant cotton bud, and that made me want to laugh and cry.

Up until tonight, the only version of me that really existed still lived at Westerham Street, still loved a boy with dark curls and bare feet and a bravery that lay somewhere beyond wisdom. But in giving him the note, I had helped her, and in doing so became something new.

"Let's burn this," I said, finally, and no one argued.

* * *

The following Friday, without telling anyone, I drove back to Westerham Street and sat waiting until 11 PM. Nobody came. I started the engine, then stopped it, unable to resist the impulse to have a quick look through the window.

The lights were on as I approached number five. I noticed something blu-tacked to the inside of the window—Dali's "Swans Reflecting Elephants," like a makeshift curtain, and in the corner a torn-out piece of notepaper with a few scrawled words:

* * *

Thank you for the warning, Olivia.

* * *

Smiling, I turned to go, knowing that I didn't need to come back anymore.

Contributors

Julian Berengaut is a retired international debt negotiator born in Poland and living currently in Bangkok, Thailand. He is the author of *The Estate of Wormwood and Honey*.

Sarah Bridgins's work has appeared in *Monkeybicycle, InDigest, Sink Review, Bluestem, Two Serious Ladies,* and *Bone Bouquet,* among other journals. Her poetry chapbook, *We Are Not Pilgrims,* was recently published by Mondo Bummer.

Like nomadic Pericú natives before him, **Matthew Dexter** survives on a hunter-gatherer subsistence diet of shrimp tacos, smoked marlin, cold beer, and warm sunshine. He is the author of the novel, *The Ritalin Orgy* (Perpetual Motion Machine Publishing 2013). His short fiction and narrative nonfiction has been published in hundreds of literary journals and dozens of anthologies. He lives in Cabo San Lucas, Mexico.

Born in Georgia (former USSR), **Regina Edwards** now lives in Brisbane, Australia, with her husband and son. She graduated from the University of Queensland with a degree in mathematics, and now works as a teacher, inflicting her enthusiasm for the subject upon high school students. When free time materializes, she writes.

Madeline ffitch was a founding member of the punk theater company The Missoula Oblongata with whom she wrote, performed, and toured to post offices, grocery stores, farms, and warehouses. Her work has appeared in *The Chicago Review* and on *Chuckwagon Press.* Her play, *Debris Upon the Forest Floor*, produced with the weaver Elspeth Vance and the musician Jordan O Jordan, was catalogued in the 2012 Emergency Index, a project of Ugly Duckling Presse. Originally from Portland, Oregon, she now lives and writes in Appalachian Ohio where she homesteads and raises ducks and her small son, Nector Vine Ballew. fitch's collection of short stories, *Valparaiso, Round the Horn*, is forthcoming from Publishing Genius.

Diane Lefer's most recent novel, *The Fiery Alphabet*, set in 18th-century Italy, Poland, and the Ottoman Empire, was published in September. Sixteen years ago, she was hired to write mitigation reports but the job evaporated before it began. She has, however, facilitated writing workshops for incarcerated youth and for men on parole. Her books include *California Transit*, which received the Mary McCarthy Prize in Short Fiction, and *The Blessing Next to the Wound*, nonfiction co-authored with Colombian exile and torture survivor Hector Aristizábal. www.dianelefer.weebly.com

Josh Ostergaard is the author of *The Devil's Snake Curve*, a book about baseball, published by Coffee House Press in 2014. He has been an urban anthropologist at the Field Museum and now works at Graywolf Press.

Joani Reese (JP) is the author of two poetry chapbooks: *Final Notes* and *Dead Letters*. Her poetry and fiction have been widely anthologized and featured in over seventy print and online venues. A senior poetry editor for Connotation Press—An Online Artifact and an annual fiction guest editor for *Scissors and Spackle*, Reese won the first Patricia McFarland Memorial Prize for her flash fiction and The Graduate School Creative Writing Award from The University of Memphis for her poetry, where she also earned her MFA. Reese lives and teaches in Texas.

Frank Roger was born in 1957 in Ghent, Belgium. His first story appeared in 1975. Since then his stories appear in an increasing number of languages in all sorts of magazines and anthologies, and since 2000, story collections are published, also in various languages. Apart from fiction, he also produces collages and graphic work in a surrealist and satirical tradition. They have appeared in various magazines and books. His work is a blend of genres and styles that can best be described as "frankrogerism," an approach of which he is the main representative. By now he has a few hundred short stories to his credit, published in about 40 languages. In 2012 a story collection in English (*The Burning Woman and Other Stories*) was published by Evertype (www.evertype.com). Find out more at www.frankroger.be.

Shya Scanlon is the author of *In This Alone Impulse, Forecast*, and *Border Run*. His novel *The Guild of St. Cooper* will be published in 2015.

An Tran is a writer from the Washington, DC area. His fiction and non-fiction has appeared or is forthcoming in the *Southern Humanities Review, Gargoyle Magazine, The Carolina Quarterly, The Good Men Project*, and *Big Lucks*, among others, and has received a "Notable" distinction from the Best American series. He is pursuing an MFA candidate at Queens University of Charlotte and he curates the Waterbear Reading Series in Arlington, Virginia.

Erika T. Wurth's novel, *Crazyhorse's Girlfriend*, has been accepted for publication by Curbside Splendor. Her collection of poetry, *Indian Trains*, was published by The University of New Mexico's West End Press. A writer of both fiction and poetry, she teaches creative writing at Western Illinois University and has been a guest writer at the Institute of American Indian Arts. Her work has appeared or is forthcoming in numerous journals including *Boulevard, Fiction, Pembroke, Florida Review, Stand, Cimarron Review, The Cape Rock, Southern California Review*, and *Drunken Boat*. She is Apache/Chickasaw/Cherokee and was raised outside of Denver.

www.ingramcontent.com/pod-product-compliance
Lightning Source LLC
Chambersburg PA
CBHW071501170626
46811CB00007B/2673